LEGAL TERMINOLOGY AND TRANSCRIPTION

LEGAL TERMINOLOGY AND TRANSCRIPTION

Marilynn K. Wallis

PRENTICE HALL, Upper Saddle River, New Jersey 07458

Library of Congress Cataloging-in-Publication Data

Wallis, Marilynn K.
Legal terminology and transcription / Marilynn K. Wallis.
p. cm.
Includes index.
ISBN 0-13-190711-5
1. Legal transcription—United States. 2. Legal secretaries—United States—Handbooks, manuals, etc. I. Title.
KF320.S4W35 1996 95-16843
340'.014—dc20 CIP

Acquisitions editor: Elizabeth Sugg
Editorial assistant: Kerri Ribik
Editorial/production supervision and interior design: Linda B. Pawelchak
Copy editor: Kathryn Beck
Cover design: Bruce Kenselaar
Production coordinator: Ed O'Dougherty

Printed in the United States of America
10 9 8 7 6 5 4 3 2 1

ISBN 0-13-190711-5

Prentice-Hall International (UK) Limited, *London*
Prentice-Hall of Australia Pty. Limited, *Sydney*
Prentice-Hall Canada Inc., *Toronto*
Prentice-Hall Hispanoamericana, S.A., *Mexico*
Prentice-Hall of India Private Limited, *New Delhi*
Prentice-Hall of Japan, Inc., *Tokyo*
Simon & Schuster Asia Pte. Ltd., *Singapore*
Editora Prentice-Hall do Brasil, Ltda., *Rio de Janeiro*

To my husband,
Bill Wallis,
without whose encouragement,
support, and assistance
I could never have completed this project

Contents

UNIT 4

UNIT 5

UNIT 6

UNIT 7

UNIT 8

UNIT 9

UNIT 10

Appendices

Preface

Assuming you bring with you basic skills, the most important asset you will have in any line of work is an understanding of what your associates are talking about. Every occupation has its own unique vocabulary. This is true whether you work on a fishing boat, in a factory, as a lumberjack, or in a law office. Since you are enrolled in the Legal Terminology and Transcription course, it is safe to assume you are not seriously interested in the vocabulary of a lumberjack, but rather in the vocabulary of a law office.

With this in mind, this text presents the most frequently used legal terms, ranging from common (in a law office) Latin words and phrases to those words with one day-to-day meaning but a different meaning when used in a legal context. There are also words or phrases used within the legal and other fields that basically have the same meaning with slight variations depending on the context. For example, *privileged communication* may mean any one of the following: one spouse cannot be ordered to testify against the other, an attorney ethically cannot divulge conversations with a client, or a priest cannot reveal confessional statements.

This text is divided into units covering the various areas of the legal profession. Unit 1 introduces you to general terminology used in all legal areas. Unit 2 relates to the court systems and will provide the proper court titles. Units 3 through 12 cover the specific areas of law, including civil court documents, litigation, family or domestic relations, wills and probate, business, real estate, and criminal law.

The goal of this course is for you to become familiar and comfortable with both the usage and the spelling of terms and expressions used on a daily basis in a legal environment. To this end there will be strong emphasis placed on definition and spelling. The dictation and transcription will include both vocabulary drills and legal document preparation.

As a novice legal secretary, I prepared a number of documents that read "the *client* states under oath . . ."; only to learn several weeks later that the dictation actually was "the *affiant* states under oath. . . ." Not knowing the word *affiant,* I heard a word I knew—*client.* This text was written to help others interested in the legal field to learn its basic vocabulary and to avoid some of the pitfalls and difficulties presented by a strange, new language.

I wish to express my gratitude to the attorneys I've worked with over the years and to my students, whose comments, suggestions, and questions have contributed greatly to the making of this book.

I would also like to thank the following reviewers: Mary Taylor; Janice Pattison, Stark Technological College; Diane Pearson, Indiana Vo-Tech College; and Jane Williams, J. Sergeant Reynolds College.

My greatest indebtedness is to the attorney I've worked with for the past 12 years. His legal knowledge, many valuable suggestions, and friendship have been an inspiration.

Marilynn K. Wallis

To the Student

This course will assist you in acquiring the ability to understand and transcribe legal documents efficiently and correctly. Although standard typewriters can be used to accomplish the purpose, the advent of word processing equipment has greatly enhanced the secretary's ability to produce excellent finished products. Attorneys are notorious for changing their minds when fine-tuning documents, and word processing capabilities simplify this process to a great extent.

There are many legal documents that may be "boilerplated"; that is, used over and over again with only minor changes, such as names, dates, and locations. With these documents, word processing capabilities are invaluable. However, for the purposes of this course, you will be encoding letters, pleadings, and other legal forms of communication from the dictation cassette tapes without benefit of pre-encoded or printed forms. If you are working with a word processing program, there are some instances in which you will be able to transcribe a document or portion of a document and then use and reuse the same material without re-encoding. Your instructor will point out these opportunities as they arise.

In the instances in this text in which words "he," "his," or any other terms usually denoting the masculine gender are used, be it understood that such terms are interchangeable with the corresponding feminine term. The inclusion of "he or she," "his or her," "himself or herself," and so on is cumbersome and makes reading and comprehension more difficult.

ORGANIZATION OF MATERIAL

Each unit contains the following sections:

1. *Vocabulary:* This section consists of terms relative to the subject matter. These are to be studied both for definition of the word or phrase and for spelling. Phonetic pronunciation is given for each word using the following phonetic key:

    ă as in pat
    ā as in pay

â as in fall, talk
ä as in far, father
âr as in care
ĕ as in pet
ē as in be
ė as in her
ĭ as in pit, pin
ī as in pie, pine
îr as in pier
ŏ as in pot, not
ō as in toe, note
ô as in paw, off
o͞o as in boot
o͝o as in took
ŭ as in cut, up
ū as in mute, few
u̇ as in pull, book
ûr as in urge
ə as in above

2. *Vocabulary-Dictation:* This section consists of a hard copy of the dictation that incorporates the vocabulary and definitions. This dictation provides an opportunity to hear the terms pronounced, reinforcement of the meanings of the words or phrases, and transcription practice. For emphasis, the words or phrases from the unit's vocabulary are underlined in the hard copy; however, this does not mean they are to be underlined in day-to-day usage.
3. *Self-test:* The self-tests will assist you in evaluating your comprehension of the vocabulary.
4. *Transcription exercises:* These letters, documents, and instruments are designed to provide reinforcement of the vocabulary and practical experience in transcribing legal material.

The book concludes with three appendices that complement the material in each unit:

1. The correct answers to the self-tests;
2. Style and format samples; and
3. Index to the vocabulary terms.

DICTATED MATERIALS

The vocabulary and exercises for the first two units are general in nature. The dictation is somewhat slower, which will give you the opportunity to become comfortable with your transcription equipment before you work with the form and structure of pleadings and other legal documents.

Punctuation and capitalization have been included in the dictation of the first four units to assist you in getting a feel for these elements in legal transcription. In the dictated materials after Unit 4, punctuation and capitalization will not be dictated, except in unusual situations. It is expected that in most instances you will be able to supply the correct punctuation and capitalization based on what has been learned to that point. Hard copies of the Vocabulary-Dictation and Exercises are provided as an aid to you in checking your transcriptions for content, punctuation, and capitalization. DO NOT REFER TO HARD COPIES BEFORE

TRANSCRIBING TAPES. If you want to practice typing, type from the hard copies. If you want to develop transcribing skills, type from the dictated material on the cassettes.

TRANSCRIPTION EVALUATION

The name of the game is "make it correct and make it pretty." In the legal field, it is of paramount importance that you "make it correct." It is impossible to overemphasize the importance of "correct." Changing one small word can change the entire meaning of a statement. If the word *the* was dictated but you transcribe it as ". . . was *a* proximate cause of the accident," you are saying that this is one of perhaps many causes. However, if you transcribe correctly and type ". . . was *the* proximate cause of the accident," you are saying that this was the *only* proximate cause.

After being as certain as humanly possible that the document is correct, use your creative abilities to make it attractive. This will enable both you and your firm to be proud of the work that goes out. An attractive document is one *without* typos, *without* obvious corrections, and *with* balanced spacing. "Balanced spacing" is signified by slightly less open space at the top of the page than at the bottom, equal margins on both sides of the page, and wider margins if there is little text (e.g., a very short letter).

In evaluating your transcriptions, use the following guide:

1. A nicely balanced, error-free document is excellent.
2. A document with one or two minor errors that have been corrected so they are not noticeable is good.
3. A document with a few errors and corrections that *might* be noticed can be considered satisfactory. "Satisfactory" will be determined to a large extent by the intended distribution of the document. If it is for interoffice distribution, less than perfect will do (but don't be sloppy—you'll embarrass both yourself and your boss). However, if it is to be filed with the Supreme Court . . .
4. A document with mistakes and obvious corrections is unsatisfactory. You need to repeat the exercises striving to produce an acceptable document.

TRANSCRIPTION TIPS

At the beginning of each class, check to assure the counter on the transcriber is set at zero. After each transcribing session, *make a note of the reading on the counter* and rewind the tape. If you do not have some indication of where you stopped transcribing, you can waste a great deal of time searching for the starting place.

Before beginning the Vocabulary-Dictation of each unit, be certain you are familiar with the pronunciation, spelling, and definitions of the terms in that unit.

Be consistent. Variations will occur from court to court, from law firm to law firm, and from attorney to attorney. For example, some firms want the names of both individuals and businesses to be typed in all caps in a legal document; others want upper and lower case. For the purposes of this class, select the style you believe is most attractive, but be consistent throughout the course.

Remember when typing legal instruments, memorandums to the file, letters, and so on that most legal documents will be filed with Acco fasteners at the top of the page. Be sure to allow a sufficient top margin for the two holes punched at the top plus the amount of paper used in folding each page over the top of the file folder.

As you listen to the transcriber, try to increase the number of words you can retain in your mind before stopping the transcriber. The ultimate goal is to type continuously with your fingers only a word or two behind the dictation. In practice this is difficult to obtain. Listen to several words, perhaps a complete phrase, stop the transcriber, and type what you have retained. Most transcribers are set to resume by playing the last word or two on the tape prior to where you stopped it. Again, listen to a phrase, strive to increase the numbers of words you can remember, stop the transcriber, type, and so on. If you miss a word or forget a word, you can always back up the transcriber and check your work.

In an office environment, you ability to maintain your typing speed at the same rate as the dictation will depend on your diligence in practice and, to a great extent, on the person doing the dictation. Some individuals speak so rapidly that you couldn't keep up if your typing speed were 120 words per minute. Others speak so slowly, stopping often to think about what they're saying, that you could write your own letter while transcribing one of theirs.

The material for this course has been dictated at a speed that is average for most persons involved with legal dictation. It will therefore provide you with practice in transcribing most dictation. In reviewing your work, try to be objective with a critical eye toward accuracy. Always put forth your best effort in terms of both accuracy and speed—never be satisfied with less.

HIGH TECH AND THE LEGAL ARENA

High technology and the legal profession represent a marriage made in heaven. Twenty years ago the two greatest expenses for a law office were the support staff and the law library, and the greatest challenge was producing the quantities of required paperwork. (Imagine life with no copier, only carbon paper; no liquid paper, only an eraser.)

Today, with the use of a computer, a modem, and a subscription to one of several on-line services, the substantial initial investment and ongoing maintenance costs of a law library are eliminated. As fringe benefits, much less space is required for book shelves and storage, and staff does not spend time inserting updates.

Regarding the support staff, when an attorney spends half of a day dictating directly to a secretary taking shorthand, in effect, an entire workday is used. Since it does involve an inefficient use of time, shorthand has become a dinosaur and will soon be extinct. Use of machine dictation provides much better utilization of time: the employer can dictate when convenient—for example, between appointments, in his car, in the evening—and the secretary can transcribe in between performing other responsibilities. Therefore, in the new high-tech age, the ability to transcribe dictation is a much more important asset than the ability to take shorthand.

Although there may still be some law offices using manual typewriters and carbon paper, they are exceedingly rare—and you would not want to work in them anyway.

Word processing equipment enables the attorney to revise and revise and revise. It enables the secretary to transcribe many documents once—to be used and reused. In the exercises you will be doing in this course, you will find a number of documents that fall into this category. Examples of mini-documents are attorney's signature block, which goes at the end of all pleadings; the certificate of service; and various forms of notarial documents. An important, very useful mini-document is the caption for a particular lawsuit or case. Once a lawsuit has been filed and the case number and court assigned, the caption remains the same throughout the duration of the case—which may be for years. Using word processor capabilities, the complete caption including cause number and court should be created as a mini-document to be "dropped in" every time a pleading is to be prepared in that case.

Even more useful from a time-saving standpoint, many basic documents can be stored for reuse with greater or lesser modification. An example is the initial pleading in a divorce action. Certain factual information, such as residence, date of marriage, date of separation, and children, if any, is required by statute. Therefore, all petitions for divorce will include these elements, allowing the attorney to dictate and the secretary to transcribe the basic form one time. From that point on, the basic form can be "dropped in" and changes made to reflect the specifics of the case. There is also software available that supplies law offices with the customary pleadings in almost every area of law.

As you go through the exercises in this text, look for mini-documents you will want to save to be reused. In a law office, as you transcribe, look for opportunities to store documents for use in the future—it will save you and the attorney a great deal of time.

There is a potential problem with the use of word processing equipment. It creates a tendency to be careless—on the part of the attorney in writing the initial drafts and on the part of the secretary in typing—because of the ease of correction. However, if word processing equipment is available, there is no excuse for anything less than virtually error-free documents with no corrections.

If a document is to be saved and reused, it is of the greatest importance to be absolutely certain it is correct when initially saved. There is a human tendency to never really focus on a document you "drop in" for use in a new document. One oil company was known to stamp envelopes directed to the "New Mexico Oil *Conservation* Commission" for over two years before anyone noticed the stamp read "New Mexico Oil *Conversation* Commission."

Although many do not yet have the necessary equipment, more and more courts are authorizing the filing of pleadings by facsimile transmission. When this becomes a common practice, the certificate of service will have to be modified to reflect that "a true and correct copy of the foregoing was this day faxed to . . . ." It is also possible to transact such routine matters as requesting a federal ID number from the IRS by means of the fax machine.

For several years, it has been possible to file your federal income tax return by electronic means—that is, one computer transmits the return to another computer, which then prints out the return. It appears only a question of time before it will be acceptable and permitted to file pleadings with the court by electronic means between law office and courthouse computers.

The high-tech possibilities are very exciting and seemingly endless. The individual who embraces the latest and greatest will not only remain at the forefront of his profession, be he attorney, law clerk, secretary, or receptionist; but he will also partake of the excitement of the future.

ELEMENTS OF LEGAL STYLE

In the legal world, there is a much greater use of commas and semicolons than in other professions. In an effort to be very specific, an attorney may include many parenthetical phrases. It is not uncommon to have a sentence that will span eight or ten typed lines.

Although the "sense of punctuation " and other elements of style may differ from office to office and attorney to attorney (and the way YOUR attorney wants to do it is *always* the RIGHT way), there are certain rules of style, especially with regard to punctuation, that usually apply. No attempt has been made in this text to cover all the rules of punctuation; what is featured here are errors that are commonly made and correct usage of expressions frequently found in legal letters and documents.

Capitalization

Act, bill, code, and so on are capitalized when used as proper nouns in titles:

TITLE	GENERAL USAGE
Civil Rights Act	an act to protect the rights of . . .
Bill of Rights	the handicapped bill of rights
Texas Property Tax Code	the tax code provides

Court is capitalized when referring to a specific judge, when naming a specific court (the 82nd District Court), or when referring to the United States Supreme Court:

The Court gave instructions to the jury.	The matter was remanded to the trial court.
In the Fifth District Court of Appeals	The appeals court denied the motion.

Constitution is capitalized only when used in the full (proper) name of a constitution or when referring to the Constitution of the United States of America:

The Constitution of the State of Texas	The state constitution established the court system.
The Constitution guarantees the right of free speech.	

A word, used alone, that refers to groups is capitalized when it is used as the shortened form of a specific group:

Texas State Bar	the Bar
Industrial Accident Commission	the Commission
Appraisal Review Board	the Board

Legal custom indicates certain phrases, particularly in pleadings, are typed using all capital letters—for example, TO THE HONORABLE JUDGE OF SAID COURT: (see Style Sample, page 196).

Numbers

Spell out the numbers zero to ninety-nine in text.
Round numbers may be spelled out (four thousand).
Use numerals in a series that contains numbers (9, 57, 110, and 217).

When typing dollar amounts in numerals, always include cents; for example, $200.00 The instructions in most writing manuals say to omit the cents on even dollar amounts; for example, $200. In legal writing the .00 is usually included to avoid the slightest possibility of confusion.

Commas

The comma, which is the smallest interruption in continuity of thought, is the most important element of punctuation for reading ease and understanding.

In a sentence containing two independent clauses joined by a coordinating conjunction (and, but, or, nor, for), a comma is usually placed before the conjunction:

> The client phoned to request an appointment, and the attorney scheduled it for the following day.

Do not use a comma before a conjunction joining the parts of a compound predicate (i.e., one subject, two verbs):

> The client phoned to request an appointment and asked that it be scheduled the following day.

A comma, or some form of punctuation, must be used preceding and following: namely, that is, for example, i.e., and e.g.

> Many people want stronger environmental laws, namely, antipollution, antismoking, and antifluorocarbons.

> The Bill of Rights guarantees individual freedoms, for example, freedom of speech.

> Having a Will assures distribution of your property according to your wishes (e.g., Cousin Suziebelle will get your diamond earrings). (Note: In this example, the punctuation preceding *e.g.* is a parenthesis and the following punctuation is a comma.)

Dash

In typeset print, a dash is a continuous line. In typescript, it consists of two hyphens without a space between the hyphens or the words preceding and following the dash.

> A court will often have two opinions—concurring and dissenting—in its written opinion.

Ellipses

An ellipsis (three periods) indicates an omission of words, phrases, or paragraphs in quoted material. (Quite often the person dictating will say, "three little dots," rather than "an ellipsis.") In typescript, ellipsis points are period dots with a space before each dot (unless the first dot is a period) and a space after the last dot if a word follows. Since the ellipsis indicates an omission in a quotation, it is always placed within the quotation marks.

An omission in the middle of a sentence:

> In conclusion the judge stated: "Before hearing this motion, the Court expects . . . to be informed of the witnesses to be called."

An omission in the middle of a sentence with punctuation immediately preceding the ellipsis:

> The judge concluded: "Before hearing this motion to suppress, . . . the Court expects a response from counsel."

If other punctuation occurs immediately before a word preceded by ellipsis points, that punctuation mark is placed before the word with the usual intervening space:

> In conclusion the judge stated: "Before ruling on this motion . . . ; and before rehearing, the Court expects supplemental briefing."

If the omission occurs after a complete sentence, there are four period dots at the end of the sentence; the first without a space after the last word is the period for the sentence; the other three indicate the ellipsis:

> The judge in giving his findings stated that "The defendant has not proved his claim. . . . Additional evidence must be presented before final ruling." (Note: two spaces before following sentence.)

Quotation Marks

Periods and commas should be placed inside quotation marks (even when the quotation marks enclose only one letter or figure):

> As the cross-examination ended, the judge remarked, "The Court will now hear the closing arguments."
>
> The client responded, "I will do as you say," but he probably does not understand the reasoning behind the request.
>
> The Court requested an additional copy of Exhibit "A."

Semicolons and colons are placed outside the quotation marks:

> The jury returned a verdict of "guilty"; however, we are going to appeal.
>
> The foreman in reading the verdict said, "We, the jury, find the Defendant guilty as charged": guilty of conspiracy, guilty of fraud, and guilty of grand theft.

Question marks and exclamation marks should be placed outside the quotation marks unless the question or the exclamation occurs within the quotation itself:

> Did you respond to his remark "I am here to give you advice—not to tell you what to do"? (Note: Question not posed within the quotation, but in the sentence as a whole.)
>
> The lawyer asked, "Do you want your entire estate to go to this charity?" (Note: Question exists only in quoted matter, not in sentence.)
>
> The lawyer leaped from his seat and screamed, "I strongly object!" (Note: Exclamation clearly belongs in the quotation rather than in the sentence as a whole.)
>
> I was furious when he stated, " I am not going to represent you"! (Note: Entire sentence is exclamatory.)

The preceding pages introduce the student to the material presented in this text. How the material was dictated, an overview of goals for transcribed documents, and suggestions to assist the student in achieving transcription proficiency were presented. As society becomes more and more computer and high-tech oriented, students will realize the importance of having such knowledge and experience.

As stated above, no attempt has been made to cover all areas of style. Those that have been addressed are the most prevalent in the legal field. It bears repeating that many attorneys have strong opinions about how they want their documents styled. Learn the basic rules and follow the generally accepted practices, but do not try to change an attorney's opinion on proper style.

As you work your way through the following material, keep in mind your overall goals:

1. To become so familiar with legal terms that you can use them (and spell them) without a second thought;
2. To become comfortable with transcription techniques and increase your transcription speed from day to day; and
3. To create legal documents that are accurate and attractive.

LEGAL TERMINOLOGY AND TRANSCRIPTION

UNIT 1

General Legal Terminology

Many terms used in various legal documents and instruments are general in nature and are not specific to a particular area of legal practice. This unit presents both general terms (e.g., forthwith) and specific terms (e.g., tort) and provides an overview of the vocabulary you are building.

VOCABULARY

adjudicate (ə-jōō′-dĭ-kāt)	To decide a matter by legal means; for example, court, mediation, arbitration.
albeit (ôl-bē′-ĭt)	Although; even though.
allegation (ăl-ĭ-gā′-shən)	A statement or charge made in a pleading which one intends to prove by legal evidence.
bankruptcy (băngk′-rŭpt-sē)	Legal status where court divides person's assets, if any, among creditors and discharges debts.
case law (kās lô)	Law based on court decisions.
citation (cite) (sī-tā′-shən [sīt])	A reference to laws or other cases concerning law applicable in current case.
common law (kŏm-ən lô)	The major source of law in the United States; based on old English law.
constitutional law (kŏn-stə-tōō′-shən-əl lô)	Law established by either federal or state constitutions as interpreted by appropriate federal or state courts.
counsel (koun′-səl)	Attorney at law.
defendant (dĭ-fĭn′-dənt)	The party being sued or tried in either civil or criminal action.

execute (ĕk′-sĭ-kyo͞ot)	To sign a legal document as required by the document; for example, before a notary public.
feasance (fē′-zəns)	The proper performance of an act (rarely used).
forthwith (fôrth′-wĭth)	Immediately, soon.
heretofore (hîr′-tə-fôr)	Previously; up to this time.
hereunto (hîr-ŭn′-to͞o)	To this matter or document.
in propria persona (in pro per) (ĭn prō′-prĭ-ä pėr-sō′-nä [ĭn prō pėr])	Latin; refers to one who represents himself without the assistance of an attorney.
jurisprudence (jo͝or′-əs-pro͞o-dəns)	The science or philosophy of law.
jurist (jo͝or′-əst)	A person who has a substantial knowledge of law and who has written extensively on legal matters; for example, judges, professors, and so on.
law (lô)	Rules of conduct applicable to all people and enforceable in court.
legal (lē′-gəl)	Authorized by law or not forbidden by law.
malfeasance (măl-fē′-zəns)	Misconduct; the performance of an illegal act, especially by government official; for example, the Chief of Police.
mandatory (măn′-də-tôr-ē)	Required, frequently by law.
misfeasance (mĭs-fē′-zəns)	Improperly doing a legal act.
nonfeasance (nŏn-fē′-zəns)	Failure to perform a duty.
per se (pûr sā)	Latin, meaning "in itself or by itself."
plaintiff (plān′-tĭf)	The party who initiates an action at law (lawsuit).
precedent (prĕs′-ə-dənt)	A judicial decision that is used as a guide in subsequent, similar cases.
statutory law (stăch′-ə-tôr-ē lô)	Law established by Congress or state legislatures.
the Bar (thə Bär)	When capitalized, refers to the legal profession as a whole.
the Court (thə Kôrt)	When capitalized, refers to the judge.
thereby (thâr-bī′)	By it; as a result of it.

therefor (thâr-fôr′)	For the thing previously mentioned; for it.
therefore (thâr′-fôr)	For that reason.
tort (tôrt)	A civil wrong (other than failure to fulfill a contract) that requires the payment of money damages as compensation for injury to person or property.
tortfeasor (tôrt-fē′-sŏr)	One who commits a tortious (wrong or devious) activity; for example, auto accident, assault.
whereas (hwâr-ăz′)	Since; in view of the fact that.

VOCABULARY-DICTATION

When a matter has been decided by legal means, it is said to have been adjudicated. The term, albeit, is an introductory phrase meaning "although or even though." A statement or charge, made in a pleading, which one intends to try to prove is an allegation. The legal status whereby a court divides a person's assets among creditors and wipes out debts is called bankruptcy. Jurisprudence is the science or philosophy of law, and a jurist is a person who has a substantial knowledge of law and who has written extensively on legal matters. Law is the term covering the rules of conduct applicable to all people and enforceable in court. For something to be legal, it must be either authorized by law or not forbidden by law. A judicial decision that is used as a guide in subsequent, similar cases is referred to as a precedent. A citation (often simply stated "cite") is a reference to laws or other cases supporting claims in a current case.

The major source of law in the United States—based on old English law—is referred to as common law. Law based on decisions reached in previously tried, similar cases is termed case law. Constitutional law is law determined by either federal or state constitutions. Law established by federal or state legislative statutes is referred to as statutory law. When capitalized, the word Court refers to the judge, and the phrase the Bar refers to the legal profession as a whole.

An attorney who represents a client in court cases is often referred to as counsel. The party who initiates an action at law (lawsuit or cause of action) is the plaintiff, and the party being sued or tried is the defendant. The Latin phrase "in propria persona" (often abbreviated in pro per) refers to one who represents himself without the assistance of an attorney.

To execute means to sign a legal document as required by the document; for example, before witnesses and/or a notary public. When something is mandatory, it is required, frequently by law. The Latin expression, per se, means "in itself or by itself."

Feasance is the proper performance of an act. Malfeasance is misconduct or the performance of an illegal act. Misfeasance is doing a legal act improperly, and nonfeasance is the failure to perform a legal duty. A tort is any civil wrong (other than failure to fulfill a contract) that requires the payment of money damages as compensation to the injured party. A tortfeasor is the one who commits a tortious (wrong or devious) activity.

There are many words commonly used in legal writing as introductory, connecting, or reference words. Their meanings may be similar and confusing or dissimilar and confusing, but either way it is important to understand how and when they are used. Among the more frequently used are:

1. <u>forthwith</u>, meaning "immediately or soon."
2. <u>heretofore</u>, meaning "previously or up to this time."
3. <u>hereunto</u>, meaning it applies "to this matter or document."
4. <u>thereby</u>, meaning "by it, as a result of it."
5. <u>therefor</u>, meaning "for the thing previously mentioned or for it."
6. <u>therefore</u>, meaning "for that reason."
   (Note: Particular attention should be paid to the difference between *therefor* and *therefore*.)
7. <u>whereas</u>, meaning "since or in view of the fact that."

SELF-TEST—UNIT 1

1. ______________________ means "since or in view of the fact that."
2. The term, ______________________, is an introductory phrase meaning "although or even though."
3. The legal status whereby a court divides a person's assets among creditors and wipes out debts is called ______________________.
4. A matter decided by legal means is said to have been ______________________.
5. ______________________ is the term covering the rules of conduct applicable to all people and enforceable in court.
6. A(n) ______________________ is the one who commits a tortious (wrong or devious) activity.
7. For something to be ______________________, it must be either authorized by law or not forbidden by law.
8. ______________________ means "for that reason."
9. A judicial decision which is used as a guide in subsequent, similar cases is referred to as a(n) ______________________.

10. A(n) ______________________ (often simply stated "________") is a reference to laws or other cases supporting claims in a current case.

11. A statement or charge, made in a pleading, which one intends to try to prove is a(n) ______________________.

12. The major source of law in the United States—based on old English law—is referred to as ______________________.

13. ______________________ is the science or philosophy of law, and a(n) ______________________ is a person who has a substantial knowledge of law and who has written extensively on legal matters.

14. Law based on decisions reached in similar, previously tried cases is termed ______________________.

15. ______________________ means it applies "to this matter or document."

16. ______________________ is law determined by either federal or state constitutions.

17. Law established by federal or state legislative statutes is referred to as ______________________.

18. When capitalized, the word ______________________ refers to the judge, and the phrase ______________________ refers to the legal profession as a whole.

19. ______________________ means "immediately or soon."

20. An attorney who represents a client in court cases is often referred to as ______________________.

21. ______________________ means "for the thing previously mentioned or for it."

22. The party who initiates an action at law (lawsuit) is the ____________ ____________, and the party being sued (civil) or tried (criminal) is the ______________________.

23. The Latin phrase "________________________" (________________________) refers to one who represents himself without the assistance of an attorney.

24. To ________________________ means to sign a legal document as required by the document; for example, before a notary public.

25. The Latin expression, ________________________, means "in itself or by itself."

26. ________________________ is the proper performance of an act.

27. ________________________ means "previously or up to this time."

28. ________________________ is misconduct or the performance of an illegal act.

29. When something is ________________________, it is required, frequently by law.

30. ________________________ is doing a legal act improperly, and ________________________ is the failure to perform a legal duty.

31. A(n) ________________________ is any civil wrong (other than failure to fulfill a contract) that requires the payment of money damages as compensation to the injured party.

32. ________________________ means "by it, as a result of it."

UNIT 1—EXERCISE 1

Letter regarding Fees

Date

Ms. Lynn K. Baldwin
Rancho Rentals, Inc.
10020 Merit Parkway
Dallas, TX 75248

Re: Structure of Legal Fees

Dear Ms. Baldwin:

Thank you for your interest in retaining our firm to handle your personal and business legal matters. In response to your question concerning our fee structure, there are several methods of billing.

If you anticipate a continuing flow of legal work related to your business, we can establish a fixed amount to be paid monthly as a retainer. This will cover all of the day-to-day, run-of-the-mill legal work and will enable you to feel free to call for diverse legal advice as the occasion arises.

On the other hand, if you anticipate needing legal work only from time to time, it would be to your advantage to employ our firm on an as-needed basis. Under this arrangement, you would be billed for time actually spent at an hourly rate, which would vary depending on the staff personnel providing the service, plus any costs.

A third possibility is the contingent-fee basis. This billing method is often used when you anticipate our firm collecting money from a third party on your behalf. This usually applies to collection matters or damage suits; for example, personal injury. Under this arrangement, you would be billed only for costs, and, upon finalization of the matter, the firm would be paid a percentage of the recovery. If there were no recovery, there would be no fee.

If you have additional questions, please do not hesitate to call.

Very truly yours,

Bruce R. Sutton

BRS:

UNIT 1—EXERCISE 2

Collection Letter

Date

Ms. Kate Williams
2761 Glen Wood Avenue
Dallas, TX 75288

Re: Rancho Rentals, Inc.
Amount Due—$3,450.00

Dear Ms. Williams:

Our firm has been retained by the above-captioned company to collect the monies owed by you for the rental of computer equipment. As you know, Rancho Rentals has made numerous efforts to work with you in the retirement of this debt. To date, you have not indicated any desire to settle this matter.

Please contact the undersigned within ten days of receipt of this letter so that settlement can be discussed. If we do not hear from you within this period, we shall have no alternative but to file suit against you for collection of the sum of $3,450.00 plus interest, court costs, and attorney's fees.

Very truly yours,

Michelle L. Underwood

MLU:

UNIT 1—EXERCISE 3

Notice of Retained Attorney

Date

Mr. Keith Anderson
1376 Forest Park Drive
Dallas, TX 75231

Re: Milo Williams vs. Keith Anderson
D/A: August 19, 19__

Dear Mr. Anderson:

We have been retained by Mr. Milo Williams in connection with injuries and property damage sustained by him as a result of an automobile accident on or about August 19, 1990. Mr. Williams has advised that you were the owner and operator of the 1988 Chevrolet van which collided with his vehicle at the intersection of Forest Lane and Abrams Road, Dallas, Texas.

If you had liability insurance coverage at the time of this accident, please deliver the enclosed copy of this letter to your insurance carrier with the request that it contact this firm. If you did not have liability insurance coverage at the time of this accident, please contact the undersigned directly so that we may discuss payment by you of Mr. William's damages.

You are hereby placed on notice that our firm has been assigned an interest in and to the claim for damages which our client has against you.

Yours very truly,

Robert B. Edwards

RBE:

UNIT 2

Federal and State Court Systems

Although the names of the courts may vary from state to state, the basic plan for the judiciary is the same and resembles a pyramid somewhat. The base of the pyramid is made up of the courts established for relatively small geographic areas, such as a municipality or county, and for hearing lesser cases such as misdemeanors and low-dollar judgments. The next level is composed of courts that are categorized by county and that have jurisdiction over more serious crimes and/or high-dollar judgments. The courts that hear matters on appeal will usually cover entire sections of a state, such as an Eastern Division, Western Division, and so on. The top of the pyramid is the state Supreme Court, which hears cases on appeal throughout the state. The examples given in this unit are for the Texas court system. The federal court system has the same basic plan: district courts for small geographic areas and appellate courts hearing cases from the district courts of several states; the highest appellate court is the United States Supreme Court.

VOCABULARY

County Court (koun'-tē kôrt)	Established by state constitution to hear county civil and criminal cases.
County Court at Law (koun'-tē kôrt ăt lô)	An additional court that may be established by the legislature to ease caseload of county court.
Court of Appeals (kôrt ŭv ə-pēlz')	Texas's interim appellate court; hears both civil and criminal cases on appeal from lower courts.
Court of Criminal Appeals (kôrt ŭv krĭm'-ə-nəl ə-pēlz')	The highest court in the Texas judicial system that hears and decides only criminal cases.
Criminal District Court (krĭm'-ə-nəl dĭs'-trĭkt kôrt)	Established in certain large urban areas to hear major criminal cases only.
dictum (dĭk'-təm)	Latin; an authoritative opinion by a judge on points other than the actual issues of the specific case.
District Court (dĭs'-trĭkt kôrt)	Established within a county; hears major criminal and civil cases.

Justice of the Peace Court
(jŭs′-tĭs ŭv thə pēs kôrt)
Hears lesser civil and criminal cases.

Municipal Court
(myōō-nĭs′-ə-pəl kôrt)
Hears cases involving violations of municipal laws.

Probate Court
(prō′-bāt kôrt)
Established to hear probate matters.

Texas Supreme Court
(Tĕk′-səs sə-prēm′ kôrt)
The highest civil court in Texas judicial system.

U.S. Court of Appeals
(U.S. kôrt ŭv ə-pēlz′)
Appellate court in the federal judicial system; hears cases appealed from lower federal courts.

U.S. District Court
(U.S. dĭs′-trĭkt kôrt)
Federal trial court; court of original jurisdiction.

U.S. Supreme Court
(U.S. sə-prēm′ kôrt)
The highest court in the federal judicial system.

VOCABULARY-DICTATION

A County Court is established by the state constitution to hear county civil and criminal cases. When the caseload of County Courts becomes too great, the legislature can establish an extra court, called a County Court at Law, to ease the caseload burden. Lesser civil and criminal cases may be heard by a Justice of the Peace Court, whereas a Municipal Court only hears cases involving violation of municipal laws or ordinances. Major criminal and civil cases within a county are heard by a District Court, whereas a Criminal District Court may be established in certain large urban areas to hear major criminal cases only. A Probate Court is established in large urban areas to hear probate matters.

Cases on appeal from lower courts are heard by the state's interim appellate court, the Court of Appeals. The highest criminal court in the Texas judicial system is the Court of Criminal Appeals, while the highest civil court is the Texas Supreme Court.

In federal trial matters, a U.S. District Court is the court of original jurisdiction. Cases appealed from lower federal courts are heard by U.S. Courts of Appeals; the highest court in the federal judicial system is the U.S. Supreme Court.

An authoritative opinion by a judge on points other than the actual issues of a specific case is a dictum.

SELF-TEST—UNIT 2

1. A minor traffic violation or a case involving the rightful ownership of a calf might be heard by a(n) ______________________.
2. The settlement of an estate or designation of a guardian is the responsibility of a(n) ______________________.
3. Violations of city ordinances are heard in a(n) ______________________.

4. Slightly more serious civil or criminal cases in a given county are heard by a(n) ________________________.

5. To ease the caseload of a county court, an extra court may be set up, which is called a(n) ________________________.

6. Major criminal and civil cases are heard in the county's ________________________.

7. A(n) ________________________ is established in certain urban areas; its purpose is to hear major criminal cases only.

8. Appeals on cases heard in courts, 4 through 7 above, may be heard in a state ________________________.

9. The highest criminal court in the Texas judicial system is the ________________________.

10. The highest civil court in the Texas judicial system is the ________________________.

11. In the federal trial system, the court of original jurisdiction is a(n) ________________________.

12. The federal judicial system appellate court that hears cases appealed from lower federal courts is a(n) ________________________.

13. The ________________________ is the highest court in the federal judicial system.

14. A judge's authoritative opinion on points or decision of a case other than the actual issues of the specific case is a Latin word: ________________________.

UNIT 2—EXERCISE 1

Texas Court System

When Texas became a republic in 1836, one of the first things that needed to be done was to draft a constitution. Inasmuch as the United States Constitution appeared to be working well, it was used as a model in developing a court system. Both the state and federal court systems are designed in tiers, with the Supreme Court being the highest state court and the highest federal court.

The lowest court in the Texas court system is the Justice of the Peace Court. The constitution provides for at least four and not more than eight justice precincts per county, unless the population is such that additional Justices of the Peace (J.P.s) would be authorized. The J.P. courts handle criminal cases, in which the penalty could be a small fine but no jail time, and civil cases, in which the claims are small. The J.P. is authorized to perform marriages and serves as coroner in any county that does not have a medical examiner.

In Texas there are two types of county courts. The first is the County Court, established by the constitution, with jurisdiction over misdemeanor criminal cases, which may have fines and jail sentences imposed, and civil cases, which have a dollar limit higher than that of Justice of the Peace courts but lower than that of the district courts. The County Court also serves as the appellate court for a J.P. court and a municipal court. The second type of county court is the County Court at Law which is a special court created by the legislature. The jurisdiction of the County Court at Law varies considerably according to the statute under which it was created.

A municipal court is authorized by statute; not by the constitution. It is neither a civil nor an appellate court. A municipal court has exclusive jurisdiction over cases involving violation of city ordinances.

The district courts have original jurisdiction in all felony criminal cases, family law matters, land title cases, contested elections, and civil cases in which the damages sued for are in excess of a certain amount. These courts also have original and appellate jurisdiction in probate matters. A district court also has the power to issue some writs.

Moving up the ladder, the next court is the Court of Appeals. All cases "brought up on appeal" from the district and county courts, both civil and criminal (except those involving the death penalty), are heard by a court of appeals. The state is divided into districts, with each district having its court of appeals.

The Court of Criminal Appeals, which hears only criminal cases, is the highest court to which a criminal appeal can be made. It is, in effect, the Supreme Court for all criminal cases.

The Supreme Court has final jurisdiction in all civil cases. It also has original jurisdiction on writs of habeas corpus and writs of mandamus.

UNIT 3

Civil Court Documents

Many terms are not exclusive to a specific area of law but are most frequently used in a certain type of court action or legal specialty. This unit presents terms which are commonly used in, or in reference to, civil court cases.

VOCABULARY

above-entitled (ə-bŭv′--ĕn-tīt′ld*)	Previously named in the caption.
above-named (ə-bŭv′--nāmd*)	Previously named in the caption or in the document.
acknowledgment (ăk-nŏl′-ĭj-mənt)	A formal statement made before an authorized person acknowledging that the document was executed of one's own free will.
affiant (ə-fī′-ənt)	The person who makes an affidavit.
affidavit (ăf-ə-dā′-vĭt)	A written statement under oath swearing to truth of statements contained therein.
caption or style (kăp′-shən or stīl)	Data required, as a title, at the beginning of a court document; includes the case title, jurisdiction, venue, docket number, and document title.
certificate of service (sər-tĭf′-ĭ-kĭt ŭv sûr′-vĭs)	A declaration that a copy of a pleading has been served (by mail or by hand) on party named therein.

*The double hyphen (--) indicates a hyphen in the word as opposed to a division between syllables.

endorsement (ĕn-dôrs′-mənt)	Information as to the nature of a legal document written on the back of the document.
et alius (ĕt ă′-lĭ-ŭs)	Latin, meaning "and others"; often abbreviated as "et al."
in re (ĭn rē)	Regarding; as regards the case of.
jurat (jo͝or′-ăt)	A clause written at end of an affidavit stating when, where, and notary before whom affidavit was sworn.
jurisdiction (jo͝or-əs-dĭk′-shən)	The right or authority of a court to hear and adjudicate lawsuits.
prayer (prā′-ər)	The closing paragraph of a pleading stating relief sought.
venue (vĕn′-yo͞o)	The geographical location where a lawsuit is tried.
verification (vĕr-ə-fə-kā′-shən)	The signed statement at end of a document alleging that statements of fact in the document are true.

VOCABULARY-DICTATION

The term, above-entitled, in a legal instrument refers to any portion or to all of the caption of that instrument. The term, above-named, refers to a person or legal entity previously named either in the caption or in the document. A formal statement made to or before an authorized person or officer stating that a document was executed of one's own free will is called an acknowledgment. An affidavit is a written statement under oath swearing to the truth of the contents therein. The person making and signing an affidavit is an affiant. At the end of an affidavit, a clause is written stating when, where, and the notary or officer before whom the affidavit was made; such clause is called a jurat. The signed statement at end of a document, attesting that statements of fact in the document are true, is called verification.

The data required, as a title, at the beginning of a court document, which includes case title, jurisdiction, venue, docket number, and document title is called the caption or style. The prayer is the closing paragraph of a pleading stating the relief sought. A certificate of service is a declaration at the end of a pleading certifying that a copy of the pleading has been served, by mail or by hand, on the party named therein. Information as to the nature of a legal document, written on the back of that document, is an endorsement.

The Latin term, et alius, means "and others"; often abbreviated as "et al." (Note that since "al." is an abbreviation of "alius," it always has a period after the "l.") In a legal document the term in re means "regarding" or "as regards the case of." A court's right or authority to hear and adjudicate a lawsuit is referred to as jurisdiction. Venue refers to the place or county in which an alleged event occurs, or in which it is determined that a court has jurisdiction.

SELF-TEST—UNIT 3

1. The jurisdiction of a court is normally based on location, or ____________ ____________.

2. A written, sworn statement is a(n) ____________________.

3. When referring to a part or to all of the caption, use the term ____________ ____________.

4. A written, sworn statement (affidavit) is made by a(n) ____________ ____________.

5. A court hears and adjudicates cases in which it holds ____________ ____________.

6. The complete Latin term meaning "and others," is ____________ ____________.

7. A notary, before formalizing a document, will get the person to make a(n) ____________________ that the signing of the document was of his/her own free will.

8. The information found written on the reverse of a legal document is called a(n) ____________________.

9. A pleading, whether by plaintiff or defendant, ends with a(n) ____________ ____________ stating the relief sought.

10. A(n) ____________________ is a clause at the end of an affidavit stating when, where, and before whom the affidavit was sworn.

11. In a legal document the term, "as regards the case of" may be abbreviated to ____________________.

12. One party to a lawsuit indicates that an adverse party was furnished with a copy of a pleading with a(n) ____________________.

13. A document is completed with a signed statement, also known as ________________________, attesting to truth therein.

14. A person or legal entity previously named in either the caption or in the document is referred to by the term ________________________.

15. The case title, jurisdiction, venue, docket number, and document title appear in the ________________________ of each court document.

UNIT 3—EXERCISE 1

Caption Style Sample and Explanation

No. ____________________

FLOWER COUNTRY CLUB, INC.,	§	IN THE DISTRICT COURT
	§	
Plaintiff,	§	
	§	
vs.	§	
	§	109TH JUDICIAL DISTRICT
DALLAS COUNTY APPRAISAL	§	
DISTRICT and APPRAISAL REVIEW	§	
BOARD OF DALLAS COUNTY	§	
APPRAISAL DISTRICT,	§	
	§	
Defendants.	§	DALLAS COUNTY, TEXAS

PLAINTIFF'S ORIGINAL PETITION

We all are familiar with the expression, "More than a pretty face." By the same token, the caption for or style of a case is more than an attractive way to entitle a cause of action. The caption immediately tells you several important things about the case.

The first item in a Texas district court caption is the number assigned by a court clerk to that particular cause of action. When the Original Petition is filed, the court clerk assigns it a number, and from that point on all pleadings filed relative to that case bear the same number.

The next important information furnished in the caption is a listing of the parties involved in the case. This information is listed on the left side of the caption and includes the names of both the plaintiff(s) and the defendant(s).

On the right side of the caption is the information concerning the court in which it is filed. The first item tells you what court it has been filed in, for example, the District Court. Immediately below this, the jurisdiction is described—109th Judicial District. Under the jurisdiction is listed the venue—Dallas County, Texas.

Last, but not least, is the title of the pleadings—what it is: "Original Petition" or "Answer to Original Petition," and so on. In one concise heading or caption, the reader is provided with a number for tracking, the parties to the action, the specific court with jurisdiction and venue, and the subject matter of the document.

UNIT 4

Litigation

Section 4A
Commencement of Lawsuit
(Petition, Answer, Cross-Complaint)

Outside of business law (contracts, agreements, corporate documents, etc.) and probate, most legal practice involves litigation or the adversarial process. "Adversarial" indicates that one or more person(s) or entity(ies) are in opposition to another person(s) or entity(ies).

VOCABULARY

answer (ăn′-sər)	A pleading made in response to allegations contained in a petition.
at issue (ät ĭsh′-o͞o)	A lawsuit ready to be heard in court when pleadings are complete.
citation (sī-tā′-shən)	A writ or process served upon a defendant notifying him that a lawsuit or cause of action has been filed and that an appearance (answer) must be made.
conform (kən-fôrm′)	Make a copy of a document identical to the original.
contributory negligence (kən-trĭb′-yə-tôr-ē nĕg′-lĭ-jəns)	Carelessness on someone's part that contributed to plaintiff's loss or injury.
counterclaim (koun′-tər-klām)	A claim by a defendant against an opposing party that arises out of the subject matter of opposing party's claim.
court docket (kôrt dŏk′-ĭt)	A record of the dates and times that cases are to be heard by the court.
cross-claim (krôs--klām)	A claim by one party against a co-party that arises out of subject matter of the original action or a counterclaim therein.
default (dĭ-fôlt′)	Loss of a suit for failure to take necessary legal steps within legally specified time limits.

docket number (dŏk′-ĭt nŭm′-bər)	The number assigned to the case by the court clerk.
grounds for (grounds fôr)	The basis or reasoning behind an action.
litigant (lĭt′-ĭ-gənt)	A party to a lawsuit; one involved in litigation.
personal service (pûr′-sən-əl sûr′-vĭs)	Personal delivery of pleadings or process upon a party to the action.
petition (pə-tĭsh′-ən)	The first document filed by the plaintiff in a legal proceeding.
pleadings (plē′-dĭnz)	The Plaintiff's Petition and the Defendant's Answer, setting forth the claims and defenses of the parties.
proximate (prŏk′-sə-mĭt)	Direct or immediate (cause of injury or damage).
statute of limitations (stăch′-ōōt ŭv lĭm-ə-tā′-shəns)	A law requiring that a cause of action be commenced within a specific period of time.
tangible damages (tăn′-jə-bəl dăm′-ĭjs)	Damages that are real or actual—an essential element of a tort.

VOCABULARY-DICTATION

The basis or reasoning behind an action is referred to as "grounds for." The first document filed by the plaintiff in a legal proceeding is the petition. Proximate means direct or immediate, as in proximate cause of an injury. Tangible damages, which are real or actual damages, are an essential element of a tort.

A defendant is served with a citation, which is a writ or process notifying him that a lawsuit has been filed and that an appearance, or answer, must be made. Personal service is personally delivering pleadings or process upon a party to the action. Any party to a lawsuit (or litigation) may be referred to as a litigant. In court proceedings, an answer is a pleading made by the defendant in response to allegations contained in a petition or claim. The Plaintiff's Petition and the Defendant's Answer, setting forth the claims and defenses of the parties, are referred to as pleadings. A case, or lawsuit, ready to be heard in court when pleadings are complete, is said to be at issue. A copy of a document made identical to the original is said to have been conformed. The court docket is a record of the dates and times that cases are to be heard by the court. The number assigned to the case by the court clerk is called the docket number.

Carelessness by someone which, in part, contributed to the plaintiff's loss or injury is termed contributory negligence. If a defendant feels he has a claim arising out of the same subject matter of the Original Petition, the defendant would file a counterclaim against the plaintiff. If the defendant believes a co-party was to blame or contributed to loss or injury as set forth in original action, the defendant would file a cross-claim. A law requiring that an action be commenced within a specific period of time is called the statute of limitations. A party who fails to take necessary legal steps within legally specified time limits is said to be in default.

SELF-TEST—UNIT 4A

1. If a defendant feels he has a claim arising out of the subject matter of the Original Petition, the defendant would file a(n) ______________________.
2. First document filed by the plaintiff in a legal proceeding is the ______ ________________.
3. ______________________, which are real or actual damages, are an essential element of a tort.
4. A defendant is served with a(n) ______________________, which is a writ or process notifying him that a lawsuit has been filed and that an appearance, or answer, must be made.
5. In court proceedings, a(n) ______________________ is a pleading made by the defendant in response to allegations contained in a petition or claim.
6. The basis or reasoning behind an action is referred to as "__________ ___________."
7. The Plaintiff's Petition and the Defendant's Answer, setting forth the claims and defenses of the parties, are referred to as ______________________.
8. A party who fails to take necessary legal steps within legally specified time limits is said to be in ______________________.
9. A case, or lawsuit, ready to be heard in court when pleadings are complete is said to be ______________________.
10. Carelessness by someone which, in part, contributed to the plaintiff's loss or injury is termed as ______________________.
11. A copy of a document made identical to the original is said to have been ______________________.
12. The ______________________ is a record of the dates and times that cases are to be heard by the court.

13. ______________________ is personally delivering pleadings or process upon a party to the action.

14. A direct or immediate cause of an injury is referred to as a(n) ______________________ cause.

15. The number assigned to the case by the court clerk is called the ______________________.

16. If the defendant believes a co-party was to blame or contributed to loss or injury arising out of the subject matter of the original action, the defendant would file a(n) ______________________.

17. A law requiring that an action be commenced within a specific period of time is called the ______________________.

18. A(n) ______________________ is a person who is engaged in a lawsuit and may be either the plaintiff or the defendant.

UNIT 4A—EXERCISE 1

Medical Authorization

MEDICAL AUTHORIZATION

This will authorize my attorneys, Sutton, Underwood & Edwards, or their agents, to inspect the original and obtain copies of all medical reports and records, X-rays and X-ray reports, hospital records, and all billings in connection with the injuries and damages that I sustained as a result of an incident which occurred on August 19 of this year.

This authorization shall also extend to any of my medical treatment, both prior to and subsequent to the date of the incident referred to above.

This authorization shall further extend to any records regarding my past and present employment.

A photostatic copy of this authorization shall be used with the same force and effect as though it were an original.

Dated this __________ day of ________________, 19____.

____

(*Instructions:* Provide a blank line for the signature of Milo Williams.)

UNIT 4A—EXERCISE 2

Certificate of Service

(*Instructions:* The following are short documents that are used frequently. If word processing equipment is available, these documents should be set up individually so they can be retrieved and "dropped into" pleadings and instruments on an as-needed basis.)

CERTIFICATE OF SERVICE

This is to certify that a true and correct copy of *Defendants' *Original Answer has been served by Certified Mail No. ______________________, Return Receipt Requested, upon *Plaintiff's Attorney of Record addressed as follows:

Mr. Richard F. Smith*
Abrams, Forest, Preston & Spring
2800 Lincoln Plaza
500 N. Akard
Dallas, Texas 75201

on this __________ day of ________________, 19____.

____
Michelle L. Underwood

(*Note:* Asterisks [*] indicate items in this form that may be changed to reflect instrument and party being served.)

Notary Block

(A simple *notary public signature block* follows.)

```
STATE OF TEXAS       §
                     §
COUNTY OF DALLAS     §

    Subscribed and sworn to before me, the undersigned au-

thority, this __________ day of ________________, 19____.


                              ______________________________
                              Notary Public, State of Texas

My commission expires:        ______________________________
                              Printed Name of Notary
______________________
```

(*Note:* This form is often referred to by attorneys as the "subscribed and sworn to" phrase.)

Jurat

(Another sworn statement, known as a *jurat,* follows.)

STATE OF TEXAS §
§
COUNTY OF DALLAS §

BEFORE ME, the undersigned authority, on this day personally appeared John Roe, who being by me duly sworn, deposed and said that he is the Attorney of Record for Valium, Inc.; that he has read the above and foregoing Defendant's Original Answer, and that the statements contained therein are within his personal knowledge true and correct.

____
John Roe

SUBSCRIBED AND SWORN TO BEFORE ME, the undersigned authority, on this __________ day of ________________, 19____.

____
Notary Public for the State of Texas

My commission expires: ______________________________
Printed Name of Notary

____

Acknowledgment

(The following is an *acknowledgment*, and, when included, is *always* part of a document or instrument, in that it acknowledges that the *foregoing* document is true and correct.)

STATE OF TEXAS §
§
COUNTY OF DALLAS §

This instrument was acknowledged before me on the ______ day of ______________, 19__, by ______________________________.

____
Notary Public for the State of Texas

My commission expires: ______________________________
Notary's Printed Name

____

UNIT 4A—EXERCISE 3

Plaintiffs' Original Petition

No. ______________________

MILO WILLIAMS and ESTHER WILLIAMS,	§	IN THE DISTRICT COURT
	§	
	§	
Plaintiffs,	§	
	§	________ JUDICIAL DISTRICT
vs.	§	
	§	
KEITH ANDERSON,	§	
	§	
Defendant.	§	DALLAS COUNTY, TEXAS

PLAINTIFFS' ORIGINAL PETITION

TO THE HONORABLE JUDGE OF SAID COURT:

COME NOW Milo Williams and Esther Williams, Plaintiffs, complaining of Keith Anderson, Defendant, and for cause of action would respectfully show the Court:

I.

Plaintiffs are now and were at all times relevant hereto husband and wife.

II.

Plaintiffs are residents of Dallas, Dallas County, Texas. Defendant is a resident of Dallas, Dallas County, Texas, and service of citation may be had upon him at 2414 Mockingbird Road, Dallas, Texas.

III.

On or about August 19, 1996, Forest Lane and Abrams Road were public roads located within Dallas County, Texas.

IV.

On August 19, 1996, Plaintiff Milo Williams was stopped at a traffic control device at the intersection of Forest Lane and Abrams Road in Dallas, Dallas County, Texas.

V.

At all times mentioned herein, Plaintiff Milo Williams was operating a 1989 Mercedes Benz vehicle (Texas license No. 429 XYZ).

VI.

At all times herein mentioned, Defendant was the owner and driver of a 1988 Chevrolet van (Texas license No. 555 ZYX).

VII.

On or about August 19, 1996, Defendant operated the said Chevrolet van in a negligent manner on Abrams Road near the intersection of Forest Lane in Dallas County, Texas, causing said motor vehicle to collide with the vehicle operated by Plaintiff Milo Williams.

VIII.

The collision and resulting damage and injuries to Plaintiffs were proximately caused by Defendant's negligence in the following respects:

1. Defendant failed to have his automobile under control;

2. Defendant failed to apply brakes in time to avoid the collision;

3. Defendant failed to drive his vehicle at a reasonable rate of speed on approaching the intersection;

4. Defendant failed to keep a proper lookout for vehicles stopped at the intersection; and

5. Defendant failed to give proper regard to other vehicles, including that of Plaintiffs.

IX.

As a direct and proximate result of the negligence of Defendant Keith Anderson in the operation of his motor vehicle, his motor vehicle was caused to collide with the rear of the 1989 Mercedes Benz being operated by Plaintiff Milo Williams, causing Plaintiff Milo Williams to be injured.

X.

As a direct and proximate result of the negligence of the Defendant, Plaintiff Milo Williams has been caused to expend sums of money for the medical care and treatment of his injuries, and in the future will be required to expend sums of money for medical treatment of his injuries.

XI.

As a direct and proximate result of the negligence of the Defendant, Plaintiff Esther Williams has been denied the services and companionship of Plaintiff Milo Williams.

XII.

Plaintiff Milo Williams has been continuously disabled from employment since the date of the accident and may in the future be disabled from employment as a result of the aforementioned injuries.

XIII.

Plaintiff Milo Williams has suffered permanent injury as a result of the negligence of the Defendant.

XIV.

Plaintiff Milo Williams has suffered a loss of earning capacity as a result of the Defendant's negligence.

XV.

Plaintiff Milo Williams has been caused to endure great pain and suffering as a result of the negligence of the Defendant.

WHEREFORE, PREMISES CONSIDERED, Plaintiffs pray for judgment against the Defendant, as follows:

1. For general damages in an unknown amount;

2. For medical and related expenses according to proof;

3. For loss of earnings and earning capacity according to proof;

4. For property damage and loss of use according to proof;

5. For loss of services and companionship;

6. For costs of suit herein;

7. For legal interest from the date of injury to the date of judgment; and

8. For such other and further relief as the Court may deem just and proper.

Dated this ________ day of ______________________,

19_____.

(*Instructions:* Provide a signature block for your attorney, as Attorney for Plaintiffs. See Style and Format Samples, page 192.)

STATE OF TEXAS §
§
COUNTY OF DALLAS §

I, Milo Williams, being first duly sworn, state:

"I am a Plaintiff in the above-entitled action. I have read the foregoing Original Petition and know the contents thereof, and I certify that the same is true of my own knowledge.

"I certify under penalty of perjury that the foregoing is true and correct."

Executed on this __________ day of ________________, 19____.

(*Instructions:* Provide a signature line for Milo Williams and the "subscribed and sworn to" by the notary.)

UNIT 4A—EXERCISE 4

Filing Letter

Date

Mr. Robert Burns
Dallas County District Clerk
Dallas County Courthouse
600 Commerce Street
Dallas, TX 75202

Re: Milo Williams and Esther Williams
vs. Keith Anderson

Dear Mr. Burns:

Enclosed are the original and two copies of Plaintiffs' Original Petition in the above-referenced cause. Please file the Original Petition and issue a Citation to serve the Defendant, Keith Anderson, at 2414 Mockingbird Road, Dallas, Texas 75225. Please forward the Citation and one copy of the Petition to Constable Jones for service.

A self-addressed, stamped envelope is enclosed for your convenience in returning a file-marked copy of the Petition to my office. Also enclosed is check no. 1234 in the amount of $196.00 covering filing costs and service.

Thank you for your attention to this matter.

Sincerely,

Michelle Underwood

MU:

Enclosures

UNIT 4A—EXERCISE 5

Defendant's Original Answer

(*Instructions:* In this exercise you will prepare for filing an Answer to Plaintiffs' Original Petition. Your firm has received from your client a copy of the Petition served on him. Remember to check the Petition to obtain the cause number and judicial district assigned to the case when you are preparing the Answer to an Original Petition [for this dictation the cause number and judicial district have been supplied]. Once a cause number and court are assigned, they are used throughout the progress of that case.)

Dictation:

No. 90-15982-C

MILO WILLIAMS and ESTHER WILLIAMS,	§	IN THE DISTRICT COURT
	§	
Plaintiffs,	§	
	§	96th JUDICIAL DISTRICT
vs.	§	
	§	
KEITH ANDERSON,	§	
	§	
Defendant.	§	DALLAS COUNTY, TEXAS

DEFENDANT'S ORIGINAL ANSWER

TO THE HONORABLE JUDGE OF SAID COURT:

NOW COMES Keith Anderson, Defendant, and would respectfully show the Court the following:

I.

Defendant denies all and singular, each and every, allegations of Plaintiffs' Original Petition, and upon final hearing hereof demands strict proof of such allegations by a preponderance of the evidence.

II.

Without waiving the foregoing, Defendant further pleads that the collision was proximately caused by the Plaintiff,

Milo Williams, in the operation of his automobile at the said time and place in the following respects:

1. In halting his vehicle in an improper lane at the intersection;

2. In not keeping a proper lookout for vehicles behind him; and

3. In stopping suddenly in a moving lane of traffic.

Each of these acts was the direct and proximate cause of the said collision and the injuries and damages alleged by Plaintiffs.

III.

Defendant reserves the right to amend at a later date.

IV.

Defendant demands a trial by jury.

WHEREFORE, PREMISES CONSIDERED, Defendant prays that upon final hearing of this cause the Plaintiffs take nothing and that the Defendant recover costs, and for such other and further relief, in law or in equity, both special and general, to which Defendant may show himself justly entitled.

Respectfully submitted,

____

CHARLES A. PRICE
State Bar ID No. 25030429
2121 Main Street
Dallas, Texas 75201
(214) 681-3551
(214) 681-3155 (Fax)

ATTORNEY FOR DEFENDANT

(*Instructions:* Insert Certificate of Service [see preceding Exercise 2] to show copy of this pleading furnished attorney for plaintiffs [see preceding Exercise 3 for name and address of plaintiffs' attorney].)

Section 4B
Development of Lawsuit (Motions, Discovery, Pretrial)

After litigation is commenced by filing of an original petition and an original answer, the attorneys proceed to prepare for trial with discovery procedures. These are various means by which each side can learn of the facts, witnesses, and information the other side plans to present at trial. Presented in this section are terms relative to motions and the discovery necessary for trial preparation.

VOCABULARY

deposition (dĕp-ə-zĭsh′-ən)	When a witness answers questions, oral or written, under oath. A verbatim transcript is prepared.
disclosure (dĭs-klō′-zhər)	Revealing all of the known facts concerning a cause of action.
enjoin (ĕn-join′)	To forbid or command by court order, usually an injunction.
interrogatories (ĭn-tə-rŏg′-ə-tôr-ēs)	A set of questions, oral or written.
motion (mō′-shən)	A written or oral request to the court for an order or ruling.
res ipsa loquitur (rēz ĭp′-să lŏ′-quĭ-tĕr)	Latin, meaning "the thing speaks for itself"; implies a presumption that if a thing happened, there was negligence involved because it normally does not happen.
subpoena (sə-pē′-nə)	A court-issued order to appear in court at a specified time.
subpoena duces tecum (sə-pē′-nə dū′-sēz tē′-kŭm)	An order requiring a witness to appear to testify and to bring specified documents.

VOCABULARY—DICTATION

The process of revealing all of the known facts concerning a cause of action is referred to as disclosure. A set of questions, oral or written, submitted to the adverse party is referred to as interrogatories. When a deposition is taken, the witness answers questions, oral or written, under oath. A verbatim transcript is prepared.

The court will issue an order, usually by an injunction, either forbidding or commanding performance of an action to enjoin a company or person relative to that specific action. A motion is a written or oral request to the court for an order or ruling. Res ipsa loquitur is a Latin phrase meaning "the thing speaks for itself." It encompasses the presumption that if a thing happened, there was negligence involved because it normally does not happen. A subpoena is a court-issued order for a person to appear in court at a specified time. An order requiring a witness to appear to testify and to bring specified documents is called a subpoena duces tecum.

SELF-TEST—UNIT 4B

1. The process of revealing all of the known facts concerning a cause of action is referred to as ____________________.
2. An order requiring a witness to appear to testify and to bring specified documents is called a(n) ____________________.
3. When a(n) ____________________ is taken, the witness answers questions, oral or written, under oath. A verbatim transcript is prepared.
4. The court will issue an order, usually by an injunction, either forbidding or commanding performance of an action to ____________________ a company or person relative to that specific action.
5. A(n) ____________________ is a written or oral request to the court for an order or ruling.
6. ____________________ is a Latin phrase meaning "the thing speaks for itself." It encompasses the presumption that if a thing happened, there was negligence involved because it normally does not happen.

7. A(n) ______________________ is a court-issued order for a person to appear in court at a specified time.

8. A set of questions, oral or written, submitted to the adverse party is referred to as ______________________.

UNIT 4B—EXERCISE 1

Defendant's First Set of Interrogatories to Plaintiffs

No. 90-15982-C

MILO WILLIAMS and ESTHER WILLIAMS,	§	IN THE DISTRICT COURT
	§	
Plaintiffs,	§	
	§	96th JUDICIAL DISTRICT
vs.	§	
	§	
KEITH ANDERSON,	§	
	§	
Defendant.	§	DALLAS COUNTY, TEXAS

DEFENDANT'S FIRST SET OF INTERROGATORIES TO PLAINTIFFS

TO: Michelle Underwood, attorney of record for Plaintiffs
Sutton, Underwood & Edwards
10375 Merriman Parkway
Dallas, Texas 75231

COMES NOW, Keith Anderson, Defendant in the above-entitled and numbered cause, and pursuant to Rule 168 of the Texas Rules of Civil Procedure submits the following Interrogatories to be answered by either or both of the Plaintiffs as they are able. You shall furnish all information called for by the Interrogatories that is available to you. The Interrogatories shall be signed and sworn by the party or parties answering them with respect to such answers as they shall make, and shall be served upon the undersigned within thirty (30) days from the date of service of these Interrogatories on your attorney of record.

You are instructed that:

(a) To the extent possible, you should answer these Interrogatories in the space provided for that purpose following each Interrogatory. Answers may be continued on separate sheets of paper attached to these Interrogatories, and identified by number.

(b) You are under a duty to amend your answers to these Interrogatories herein if, between the time the answers are served and the time of trial or hearing, you obtain information on the basis of which you know the information was incorrect when made or you know the answer, though correctly made, is no longer true and the circumstances are such that a failure to amend the answer is, in substance, a knowing concealment.

DEFINITIONS

Any reference to "Plaintiffs" herein shall mean the Plaintiffs named in the captioned lawsuit.

Any reference to "you or your" shall mean the "Plaintiff" or the "Plaintiffs."

The term "Document(s)" means and includes all originals and non-identical copies of any papers, estimates, medical reports, photographs, or video tapes from which information can be obtained relative to this cause of action.

The term "person" shall mean the plural as well the singular and includes: natural persons, corporations, firms, associations, partnerships, joint ventures, or any other form of legal business entity; governmental agencies, departments, units, or any subdivisions thereof.

To "identify" a person shall include a statement of the following, where applicable:

(1) The full name of the person; and

(2) The person's present business and residence addresses and telephone numbers, if known; if not known, then his or her last known business and residence addresses and telephone numbers.

INTERROGATORIES

INTERROGATORY NO. 1:

If you claim general damages, then identify the source of the valuation of damages sustained and all persons with personal knowledge of such damage and valuation.

ANSWER:

INTERROGATORY NO. 2:

With respect to medical and related expenses, identify in detail the expenses which were incurred and attach documents substantiating such expenses.

ANSWER:

INTERROGATORY NO. 3:

Describe in detail how the Plaintiffs arrived at a value for the damage to Plaintiffs' vehicle and for loss of use. Attach all documents substantiating such damage or costs directly related to loss of use.

ANSWER:

INTERROGATORY NO. 4:

Identify all professional persons, employees or consultants for the Plaintiffs who participated in gathering or evaluating information regarding Plaintiffs' damages, either to their persons or to their property.

ANSWER:

INTERROGATORY NO. 5:

Identify with respect to each person identified in the preceding Interrogatory all documents utilized by the persons in appraising damages.

ANSWER:

INTERROGATORY NO. 6:

Identify all persons you will call as witnesses at trial.

ANSWER:

INTERROGATORY NO. 7:

With respect to each witness identified in answer to the preceding Interrogatory, state:

(a) The subject matter to which the witness is expected to testify;

(b) The substance of the facts and opinions to which the witness is expected to testify;

(c) The witness's qualifications; and

(d) The identity of each document that relates or pertains to the substance of the facts and opinions to which the witness is expected to testify.

ANSWER:

(a)

(b)

(c)

(d)

Respectfully submitted,

____

CHARLES A. PRICE
State Bar ID No. 25030429
2121 Main Street
Dallas, Texas 75201
(214) 681-3551
(214) 681-3155 (Fax)

ATTORNEY FOR DEFENDANT

CERTIFICATE OF SERVICE

This is to certify that a true and correct copy of the above and foregoing instrument has been forwarded to all counsel of record in accordance with the Rules of Civil Procedure on this the __________ day of ________________, 19____.

____

Charles A. Price

UNIT 5

Litigation—Trial

There are many steps between the initial filing of a lawsuit and the completion of the litigation. After all discovery procedures have been completed, and if the case cannot be settled out of court, the next phase is a trial on the merits. This unit presents terms that may arise during selection of a jury and presentation of evidence.

VOCABULARY

admissible (ăd-mĭs′-ə-bəl)	Evidence that is material, relevant, and proper; therefore, may be presented during trial.
challenge for cause (chăl′-ənj fôr kôz)	To object to a juror for a specified reason.
corroborative (kə-rŏb′-ə-rā-tĭv)	Confirming or supporting an allegation.
evidence (ĕv′-ə-dəns)	Testimony, exhibits, or other matters presented during a trial in order to prove the allegations.
exhibit (ĕg-zĭb′-ĭt)	Any document or object presented as evidence in the trial. Must be accepted by the court before being admitted as evidence.
hearsay (hîr′-sā)	Not known by personal knowledge; learned from others.
immaterial (ĭm-ə-tîr′-ē-əl)	May be logically related to the matter in question, but doesn't affect the outcome.
impeach (ĭm-pēch′)	To prove that a witness cannot or should not be believed.
irrelevant (ĭ-rĕl′-ə-vənt)	Not logically related to the matter in question.
mistrial (mĭs-trī′-əl)	An invalid trial either because of improper proceedings or a hung jury.

peremptory challenge (pə-rĕmp′-tə-rē chăl′-ənj)	The right to eliminate a juror for no stated reason.
perjury (pûr′-jə-rē)	Intentionally or knowingly giving false testimony under oath either in court or on deposition.
plenary trial (plē′-nə-rē trī′-əl)	A complete and formal trial.
quash (kwŏsh)	Set aside; annul.
rebuttal (rĭ-bŭt′l)	An attempt to disprove or discredit evidence or oral argument.
testimony (tĕs′-tə-mō-nē)	Formal statements made under oath concerning facts known to the person regarding a case.
voir dire (vwȧr dēr′)	French; the preliminary interrogation of prospective jurors in the jury selection process.

VOCABULARY-DICTATION

A French expression used in our courts today that means the preliminary interrogation of prospective jurors in the jury selection process is voir dire. To object to a juror for a specified reason, such as being a personal friend of one of the parties, is a challenge for cause. Attorneys are allowed *x* number of peremptory challenges, which is the right to eliminate a juror for no stated reason.

A plenary trial is a complete and formal trial. A mistrial is an invalid trial either because of improper proceedings or a hung jury.

Evidence includes testimony, exhibits, or other matters presented during a trial to prove the allegations. Evidence deemed immaterial may be logically related to the matter in question, but doesn't affect the outcome. Evidence considered irrelevant is not even logically related to the matter in question.

Formal statements made under oath concerning facts personally known to an individual regarding a case is that person's testimony. Testimony that confirms or supports an allegation or allegations of either party is corroborative of that allegation. If some alleged fact is not known by the personal knowledge of the witness or is learned from others, it is hearsay and is inadmissible.

Any document or object presented as evidence in the trial is labeled an exhibit. However, it must be accepted by the court before being admitted as evidence.

Evidence that is material, relevant, and proper is admissible and may, therefore, be presented during trial. An attorney may attempt to impeach a witness in an effort to prove that the witness cannot or should not be believed. If the witness is guilty of perjury whereby he intentionally or knowingly gives false testimony under oath either in court or on deposition, a motion is made to quash, or set aside and annul his testimony.

After one attorney summarizes his case, opposing counsel may offer a rebuttal, or possible contrary evidence, in an attempt to disprove or discredit evidence.

SELF-TEST—UNIT 5

1. Attorneys are allowed *x* number of ________________________, which is the right to eliminate a juror for no stated reason.
2. A witness is guilty of ________________________ if he or she intentionally or knowingly gives false testimony under oath either in court or on deposition.
3. A trial that is invalid either because of improper proceedings or a hung jury is called a(n) ________________________.
4. Testimony or evidence offered in ________________________ is presented in an attempt to disprove or discredit evidence.
5. ________________________ includes testimony, exhibits, or other matters presented during a trial to prove the allegations of the parties.
6. A French expression used in our courts today that means the preliminary interrogation of prospective jurors in the jury selection process is ________________________.
7. A(n) ________________________ is a complete and formal trial.
8. Formal statements made under oath concerning facts personally known to an individual regarding a case is that person's ________________________.
9. Evidence deemed ________________________ may be logically related to the matter in question, but doesn't affect the outcome.
10. To set aside or annul a witness's testimony is to ________________________ the testimony.
11. If some alleged fact is not known by the personal knowledge of the witness or is learned from others, it is ________________________ and is inadmissible.

12. Any document or object, accepted by the court, presented as evidence in the trial, is labeled a(n) ______________________.

13. Once deemed material, relevant, and proper by the court, evidence is considered ______________________ and may, therefore, be presented during trial.

14. Evidence considered not even logically related to the matter in question is ______________________.

15. An attorney may attempt to ______________________ a witness in an effort to prove that the witness cannot or should not be believed.

16. Testimony that confirms or supports an allegation or allegations of either party is ______________________ of that allegation.

17. Objecting to a juror for a specified reason is a(n) ______________________.

UNIT 5—EXERCISE 1

Motion for Continuance

NO. 89-22401

THE WILD ROSE COMPANIES,	§	IN THE DISTRICT COURT
	§	
Plaintiff,	§	
vs.	§	
	§	78TH JUDICIAL DISTRICT
DALLAS COUNTY APPRAISAL	§	
DISTRICT, ET AL,	§	
	§	
Defendants.	§	DALLAS COUNTY, TEXAS

MOTION FOR CONTINUANCE

TO THE HONORABLE JUDGE OF SAID COURT:

NOW COME the attorneys for Plaintiff and Defendants and file this Motion for Continuance, and in support thereof would respectfully show the Court:

I.

The primary issue in this cause is the determination of the true boundary line between Collin County and Dallas County as it relates to the property of Plaintiff set forth in the Original Petition. At this time both Collin County and Dallas County and taxing units within each county claim a portion of the property of Plaintiff lies within such taxing jurisdictions. The attorneys for the parties understand that the counties are seeking to determine the correct boundary line and once such boundary line is agreed upon by the counties, the issues in this case can be resolved by the parties.

II.

A continuance of this matter is not sought for delay, but for the purpose of allowing the officials of Dallas County and Collin County to determine the correct boundary line of the counties.

WHEREFORE, the parties respectfully request a continuance of this matter.

<table>
<tr><td>Respectfully submitted,

ADAMS, BARNES, & CALHOUN

By ______________________
Peter G. Adams

Bar Card #15666000
1800 Lincoln Plaza
Dallas, Texas 75201
(214) 299-4533
Fax No. (214) 299-4590

ATTORNEY FOR DEFENDANT</td>
<td>Respectfully submitted,

SUTTON, UNDERWOOD, & EDWARDS

By __________________________
Signature Block
for your attorney

ATTORNEY FOR PLAINTIFF</td></tr>
</table>

UNIT 5—EXERCISE 2

Order Granting Motion for Continuance

NO. 89-22401

THE WILD ROSE COMPANIES,	§	IN THE DISTRICT COURT
	§	
Plaintiff,	§	
VS.	§	
	§	78TH JUDICIAL DISTRICT
DALLAS COUNTY APPRAISAL	§	
DISTRICT, ET AL,	§	
	§	
Defendants.	§	DALLAS COUNTY, TEXAS

ORDER GRANTING MOTION FOR CONTINUANCE

On this the _________ day of September, 1996, came on to be heard the Motion for Continuance filed herein by the attorneys for Plaintiff and Defendants. After hearing argument of counsel, the Court is of the opinion that such Motion is proper and should be granted.

IT IS THEREFORE ORDERED, ADJUDGED AND DECREED that the Motion for Continuance is hereby granted.

____
Barry Hallerman
District Judge
78th District Court
Dallas County, Texas

UNIT 5—EXERCISE 3

Certificate of Readiness

No. 90-15982-C

MILO WILLIAMS and ESTHER WILLIAMS,	§	IN THE DISTRICT COURT
	§	
	§	
Plaintiffs,	§	
	§	96th JUDICIAL DISTRICT
vs.	§	
	§	
KEITH ANDERSON,	§	
	§	
Defendant.	§	DALLAS COUNTY, TEXAS

CERTIFICATE OF READINESS

I, Michelle L. Underwood, attorney of record for Plaintiffs in the above-entitled and numbered cause, do hereby certify, in accordance with the local rules for the setting of cases, that the above cause is ready for trial, that the appearance date is passed and/or answer filed, and that all discovery procedures have been completed by the undersigned.

I further request that this certificate be filed and noted on the docket of said cause and on the jury book.

Dated this __________ day of ________________, 19____.

Respectfully submitted,

Signature Block

(*Instruction:* Insert Certificate of Service)

UNIT 5—EXERCISE 4

Motion for Preferential or Special Setting

No. 90-15982-C

MILO WILLIAMS and ESTHER WILLIAMS,	§	IN THE DISTRICT COURT
	§	
	§	
Plaintiffs,	§	
	§	96th JUDICIAL DISTRICT
vs.	§	
	§	
KEITH ANDERSON,	§	
	§	
Defendant.	§	DALLAS COUNTY, TEXAS

MOTION FOR PREFERENTIAL OR SPECIAL SETTING

TO THE HONORABLE JUDGE OF SAID COURT:

COME NOW, Plaintiffs in the above-entitled and numbered cause and would request the following:

I.

That the trial of this cause, which has been duly certified for trial, be specially set for trial for the week of ________________________________.

II.

Plaintiffs would respectfully show for reason thereof that Plaintiffs and witnesses are all from out of state, and undue inconvenience would result if this case were not specially set for the time requested.

Respectfully submitted,

Signature Block

(for Plaintiffs' Attorney)

(*Instruction:* Insert Certificate of Service for service on Defendant's attorney.)

UNIT 6

Litigation—Conclusion (Verdicts and Judgments)

After completion of the presentation of evidence, the Court or jury will be in a position to render a decision in the matter, which will terminate the lawsuit unless it is appealed. The terms presented in this unit relate to the final stages of litigation.

VOCABULARY

acquittal (ə-kwĭt′l)	A verdict that declares a person innocent of a crime.
charge to the jury (chärj to͞o thə jo͞or′-e)	Instructions as to applicable law, which are given by the Court to the jury before it begins deliberation.
contempt of court (kən-tĕmpt′ ŭv kôrt)	Disregard of a court order, which is punishable by fine, imprisonment, or both.
decree (dĭ-krē′)	An official decision or order made by a court.
deliberations (dĭ-lĭb-ə-rā′-shəns)	The process of jury discussions pursued in an effort to reach a verdict.
exonerate (ĕg-zŏn′-ə-rāt)	To prove or declare a person not guilty of charges made against him.
interlocutory (ĭn-tər-lŏk′-yə-tôr-ē)	Temporary relief granted by a court pending final judgment.
irreparable (ĭ-rĕp′-ər-ə-bəl)	So great a loss or injury that it cannot be properly compensated for or made right.
jointly and severally (joint′-lē ənd sĕv′-ər-əl-lē)	Collectively and individually.
judgment (jŭj′-mənt)	The decision of the court.
nonsuit (nŏn-so͞ot′)	An action by the plaintiff to terminate litigation.

opinion (ə-pĭn′-yən)	A statement giving the judge's reasoning that resulted in the decision made in a case.
order (ôr′-dər)	A legal ruling; also a written command made by a court.
pendente lite (pĕn-dĕn′-tē lī′-tē)	Latin, meaning "pending the suit"; litigation in process.
per curiam (pûr kū′-rĭ-ăm)	Latin, meaning "by the court"; an opinion given by the entire court.
prima facie (prī′-mə fā′-shē)	Latin, meaning "at first view"; evidence that is sufficient unto itself to be considered proof unless contrary evidence is introduced.
res judicata (rēz jū-dĭ-kā′-tă)	Latin, meaning "a thing decided"; a matter that has been decided in a court of law.
restraining order (rĭ-strān′-ĭng ôr′-dər)	A court order stating that a person or group cease an action, often for a specified period of time.
sequestered (sĭ-kwĕs′-tərd)	Latin, meaning "secluded"; may apply either to witnesses or evidence during trial, or to the seclusion of the jury pending a verdict.
stare decisis (stā′-rĕ dĕ-sī′-sĭs)	Latin, meaning "let the decision stand"; used relative to a court following precedents in deciding a case.
summary judgment (sŭm′-ə-rē jŭj′-mənt)	A judgment by a court considering <u>only</u> written pleadings and briefs of parties.
verdict (vûr′-dĭkt)	The jury's decision after hearing the evidence presented in a trial.
with prejudice (wĭth prĕj′-ə-dĭs)	Dismissal with no right to bring suit on the same matter at any future time.
without prejudice (wĭth-out′ prĕj′-ə-dĭs)	Dismissal with right to bring suit on the same matter at a later date, if desired.
writ (rĭt)	A special type of court order requiring performance or nonperformance of specific action.

VOCABULARY-DICTATION

A judgment by a court considering only written pleadings and briefs and attorneys' arguments is called a <u>summary judgment</u>. A cause of action dismissed <u>with prejudice</u> has been dismissed with no right to bring suit on the same matter at any future time. If the cause is dismissed <u>without prejudice</u>, either party has the right to bring suit on the same matter at a later date, if desired.

An <u>order</u> is an interim legal ruling. It is an oral or written command made by a court to do or not to do something. It is not a judgment. A <u>judgment</u> is the final decision of the court. The judgment is often referred to as a <u>decree</u>, which is an official decision or order made by a court. If the relief granted is temporary pending the final judgment of the court, it is referred to as an <u>interlocutory</u> decree. The court may issue a <u>restraining order</u> stating that a person or group cease an action, often for a specified period of time. A writ is a special type of court order requiring performance or nonperformance of a specific action.

If an individual disregards a court order, the judge can find him in contempt of court—punishable by fine, imprisonment, or both at the sole discretion of the court. If the plaintiff wishes to terminate the litigation, he files a nonsuit.

After the judge has considered his decision, he quite often will write an opinion, which is a statement that gives the judge's reasoning behind his decision. Written opinions are generally given on an appellate level.

The charge to the jury is a set of instructions given by the Court regarding the law that is applicable to the particular case. The "charge" is given to the jury before it begins deliberations. After receiving the charge, the jury begins its deliberations, which is the process of discussion by the jury pursued in an effort to reach a verdict. A decision reached by a jury, after hearing the evidence in a trial and after due deliberations, is called the verdict. If the jury declares a person innocent of a crime, the verdict is for acquittal.

When it is proven or declared that a person is not guilty of charges made against him, he is said to have been exonerated. If one suffers irreparable damages, the loss or injury is considered so great that it cannot be properly compensated for or made right regardless of the outcome of the case. Defendants may be found liable jointly and severally, which means they are collectively responsible, and each one is individually responsible.

There are many Latin phrases commonly used in the legal field. Among them is pendente lite, which literally means "pending the suit." This applies to a temporary order given pending the final decision. Per curiam is a Latin phrase that means "by the court" and refers to an opinion given by the entire court; for example, an appellate court in which several judges may hear the case. Prima facie is a Latin term that means "at first view." This is evidence that is sufficient unto itself to be considered proof unless contrary evidence is introduced. Res judicata, another Latin phrase, means "a thing decided." This phrase is used to refer to a matter that has previously been decided in a court of law. When a person speaks of sequestered, he means "secluded." This may apply to witnesses or evidence during trial or to the seclusion of the jury pending a verdict. The Latin term stare decisis means "let the decision stand." This term is used to refer to a court following precedents in deciding a case. In other words, the court is relying on a prior decision(s) as the proper decision rather than charting new territory.

SELF-TEST—UNIT 6

1. A cause of action dismissed ______________________ has been dismissed with no right to bring suit on the same matter at any future time.
2. A Latin term, ______________________, means "let the decision stand."
3. A Latin phrase that literally means "pending the suit" is ____________ ____________.

4. A(n) ______________________ is an interim legal ruling. It is an oral or written command made by a court to do or not to do something.
5. Plaintiff may file a(n) ______________________ to terminate the litigation.
6. If the cause is dismissed ______________________, either party has the right to bring suit on the same matter at a later date.
7. If the relief granted is temporary pending the court's final judgment, it is said to be a(n) ______________________ decree.
8. A(n) ______________________ is a special type of court order requiring performance or nonperformance of a specific action.
9. A statement that gives the judge's reasoning behind his decision is called a(n) ______________________.
10. A judgment by a court considering only written pleadings and briefs of the parties and attorneys' arguments is called a(n) ______________________.
11. The ______________________ is a set of instructions given by the Court regarding the law that is applicable to the particular case.
12. A decision reached by a jury, after hearing the evidence in a trial and after due deliberations, is called the ______________________.
13. A(n) ______________________ is a court order stating that a person or group cease an action, often for a specified period of time.
14. If the jury declares a person innocent of a crime, the verdict is for ______________________.
15. ______________________ is Latin meaning "at first view."
16. When it is proven or declared that a person is not guilty of charges made against him, he is said to have been ______________________.
17. ______________________ is a Latin phrase that means "a thing decided."
18. If one suffers ______________________ damages, the loss or injury is

considered so great that it cannot be properly compensated for or made right.

19. The process by which a jury reaches a verdict is called ____________ ____________.

20. If an individual disregards a court order, he may be held in ____________ ____________.

21. Defendants may be found ________________________ liable, which means they are collectively and individually responsible.

22. A(n) ________________________ is the final decision of the court.

23. The judgment is often referred to as a(n) ________________________, which is an official decision or order made by a court.

24. ________________________ is a Latin phrase meaning "by the court" and refers to an opinion given by the entire court.

25. During a trial, the term ________________________ would refer to witnesses, evidence, or the jury as secluded.

UNIT 6—EXERCISE 1

Plaintiff's Requested Special Issues

No. 90-17352-A

WILLIAM B. ROBERTSON,	§	IN THE DISTRICT COURT
	§	
Plaintiff,	§	
	§	
vs.	§	33rd JUDICIAL DISTRICT
	§	
MONROE MACHINERY, INC.,	§	
	§	
Defendant.	§	DALLAS COUNTY, TEXAS

PLAINTIFF'S REQUESTED SPECIAL ISSUES NUMBERS 1-3

Plaintiff in the above-named and numbered cause respectfully requests the Court that the following special issues be submitted to the jury:

Issue #1: Was the Monroe Hay Baler that was the subject of this suit defectively designed?

You are instructed that a "defectively designed" product is one which is unreasonably dangerous as designed, taking into consideration the utility of the product and the risk involved in its use.

Answer: "It was" or "It was not."

Answer: ____________________

If you have answered Issue #1 "It was," then answer Issue #2. If you have answered "It was not," do not answer Issue #2.

Issue #2: Was the defectively designed Monroe Hay Baler a producing cause of the occurrence in this lawsuit?

You are advised that there may be more than one producing cause of an occurrence. A producing cause is an efficient, exciting, or contributory cause within a natural sequence, to the damages complained of.

Answer: "It was" or "It was not."

Answer: ____________________

Issue #3: At the time Monroe Machinery, Inc. sold the hay baler in question, did it fail to give adequate warnings of the dangers or adequate instructions for safe use with respect to the product?

To be adequate, a warning must be in a form to catch the attention of the "reasonably prudent man" and to be understandable to the ordinary user in regard to the nature and extent of the danger.

Answer: "It was" or "It was not."

Answer: ____________________

Respectfully submitted,

Signature Block

ATTORNEY FOR PLAINTIFF

The foregoing special issues were:

Submitted: ______________________

Refused and exceptions allowed: ___________________________

Modified as follows: ______________________________________

____

DATE: ____________________ ___________________________

JUDGE

UNIT 6—EXERCISE 2

Motion for Judgment on the Verdict

No. 90-15982-C

MILO WILLIAMS and ESTHER WILLIAMS, Plaintiffs, vs. KEITH ANDERSON, Defendant.	§ § § § § § § § § §	IN THE DISTRICT COURT 96th JUDICIAL DISTRICT DALLAS COUNTY, TEXAS

MOTION FOR JUDGMENT ON THE VERDICT

COME NOW Plaintiffs in the above-titled and numbered cause and would show the Court the following: That the findings of the jury, in response to the special issues submitted to them, entitle Plaintiffs to judgment against Defendant, Keith Anderson, as follows:

Plaintiff Milo Williams in the amount of $27,450.00;

Plaintiff Esther Williams in the amount of $5,000.00.

THEREFORE, Plaintiffs pray that the Court render such judgment.

Respectfully submitted,

Signature Block

(*Instruction:* Prepare the Certificate of Service.)

UNIT 6—EXERCISE 3

Order

CAUSE NO. C-36,848

WALLACE PARADISE CORPORATION	§	IN THE DISTRICT COURT
	§	
Plaintiff,	§	
	§	
vs.	§	142ND JUDICIAL DISTRICT
	§	
DALLAS CENTRAL APPRAISAL DISTRICT	§	
and APPRAISAL REVIEW BOARD OF	§	
DALLAS CENTRAL APPRAISAL DISTRICT,	§	
	§	
Defendants.	§	DALLAS COUNTY, TEXAS

ORDER

On the 23rd day of January, 19__, came on to be heard the Motion of Wallace Paradise Corporation to Strike the Summary Judgment Affidavit of Ralph Carter in the First Amended Motion for Summary Judgment of Dallas Central Appraisal District in the above captioned and numbered cause and after having considered the Affidavit of Ralph Carter, the Motion of Wallace Paradise Corporation and argument of counsel, the Court finds that the Motion should be denied.

It is therefore ORDERED, ADJUDGED, and DECREED that the Motion of Wallace Paradise Corporation to Strike the Summary Judgment Affidavit of Ralph Carter in the First Amended Motion for Summary Judgment by Dallas Central Appraisal District is denied.

Signed this __________ day of ________________, 19____.

____
Pat R. Lyons, Judge
142nd Judicial District Court

UNIT 7

Litigation—Appeals

After a verdict or judgment has been rendered and entered, either side in a civil case can appeal the decision. In a criminal case, only the defendant can appeal a lower court's decision. Although some terms in this unit may be encountered at earlier stages of litigation, most are directly related to the appeal process.

VOCABULARY

abrogate (ăb′-rō-gāt)	To abolish or annul; for example, to void an order of a lower court.
amicus curiae (ă-mī′-kŭs kū′-rĭ-ē)	Latin; meaning "friend of the court"; someone not a party to the lawsuit who has knowledge of the subject matter and submits information to the court.
appeal (ə-pēl′)	To refer a decision of one court to a higher court for review.
appellant (ə-pĕl′-ənt)	The party appealing to a higher court.
appellee (ă-pə-lē′)	The defending party in a case being appealed.
brief (brēf)	A document that reviews statutes and court decisions and that is submitted to a court in support of a legal position.
compensatory damages (kəm-pĕn′-sə-tôr-ē dăm′-ĭjs)	Damages equal to but not exceeding the amount of actual loss.
damages (dăm′-ĭjs)	An amount of money awarded to one who was injured by another.
injunction (ĭn-jŭngk′-shən)	A writ issued by a court commanding a person to do or not to do something.

mandamus (măn-dā′-məs)	Latin; a writ issued by a higher court to a lower court commanding that a certain thing be done.
redress (rĭ-drĕs′)	To correct a wrong; to provide satisfaction or relief, other than money damages.
remanded (rĭ-mănd′-ĕd)	Sent back; refers to a case that is returned or sent back to a lower court with instructions for further action.
reverse (rĭ-vûrs′)	To set aside; most often by an appellate court with regard to the judgment of a lower court.
stay (stā)	A delay or stopping of a legal proceeding by the court.
supersedeas (sōō-pər-sē′-dē-əs)	Latin; a writ issued by a judge to stay a legal proceeding.
transcript (trăn′-skrĭpt)	Official copy of the original proceedings in a court.
trial de novo (trī′-əl də nō′-vō)	A new trial of a cause of action by a court as though the matter had not previously been considered by a court or in an administrative hearing.
writ of certiorari (rĭt ŭv sûr-shē-ə-râr′-ē)	An order by an appeals court requiring that a matter from a lower court be brought before it for review.

VOCABULARY-DICTATION

An amount of money awarded to one who was injured by another is referred to as damages. Compensatory damages are damages equal to but not exceeding the amount of actual loss. To redress, or correct, a wrong is to provide satisfaction or relief, other than money damages.

A writ issued by a court commanding a person to do or not to do something is called an injunction. If a decision of a lower court is reversed, it is set aside; and, most often, it is remanded, or sent back, to the trial court for a new trial. A stay is the delay or stopping, by the Court, of a legal proceeding. A writ of supersedeas (Latin) is a writ issued by a judge to stay a legal proceeding. There are many reasons to order a transcript, which is an official copy of the original proceedings in a court.

A new trial, or trial de novo, is the hearing of a cause of action by a court as though the matter had not been considered previously.

There are many terms that primarily apply to, or are used in, the appellate courts. To abrogate means to annul or declare void—for example, an order of a lower court. Amicus curiae is a Latin phrase that means "friend of the court" and identifies someone who is not a party to the lawsuit, but who has knowledge of the subject matter and submits information to the court. If either party in a civil suit is not satisfied with the judgment of a lower court, he may appeal, or refer, a decision of one court to a higher court for review. The party who files the appeal is then the appellant. The defending party in a case being appealed is the appellee. A brief is a document that reviews statutes and court decisions and that is submitted to a court in support of a legal position.

A writ of certiorari is an order by an appeals court requiring that a matter from a lower court be brought before it for review. Mandamus, a Latin word, refers to a writ issued by a higher court to a lower court commanding that a certain thing be done.

SELF-TEST—UNIT 7

1. ______________________ is a Latin word referring to a writ issued by a higher court to a lower court commanding that a certain thing be done.
2. There are many reasons to order a(n) ______________________, which is an official copy of the original proceedings in a court.
3. ______________________ are damages equal to but not exceeding the amount of actual loss.
4. The party who files the appeal is the ______________________.
5. A writ issued by a court commanding a person to do or not to do something is called a(n) ______________________.
6. If either party in a civil suit is not satisfied with the judgment of a lower court, he may ______________________, or refer, a decision of one court to a higher court for review.
7. A(n) ______________________ is an order by an appeals court requiring that a matter from a lower court be brought before it for review.
8. A(n) ______________________ is the delay or stopping of a legal proceeding by the Court.
9. A(n) ______________________ is a document that reviews statutes and court decisions and that may be submitted to a court in support of a legal position.
10. An amount of money awarded to one who was injured by another is referred to as ______________________.

11. A new trial, or ______________________, is the hearing of a cause of action by a court as though the matter had not been considered previously.

12. To ______________________, or correct, a wrong is to provide satisfaction or relief, other than money damages.

13. ______________________ is a Latin phrase that means "friend of the court" and identifies someone who is not a party to the lawsuit, but who has knowledge of the subject matter and submits information to the court.

14. A writ of ______________________ (Latin) is a writ issued by a judge to stay a legal proceeding.

15. The defending party in a case being appealed is the ______________________.

16. If a decision is ______________________, it is set aside or annulled.

17. To ______________________ means to abolish or declare void—for example, an order of a lower court.

18. If an appeals court sends a case back to a lower court for rehearing or some other action, the case is said to have been ______________________ to the lower court.

UNIT 7—EXERCISE 1

Indices to Pleadings

<u>Index to Defendants' Pleadings</u>

TITLE OF DOCUMENT	DATE FILED
1. Original Petition Filed	5-18-96
2. Agreed Order Extending Time to 9-6-96 to Respond to Request for Admissions	8-22-96
3. Answer to Defendants' First Request for Admissions	9-1-96
4. Plaintiff's Motion for Summary Judgment	11-18-96
5. Plaintiff's First Amended Original Petition	12-2-96
6. Plaintiff's Original Answer to Defendants' Original Counterclaim Petition	12-2-96
7. Plaintiff's First Amended Motion for Summary Judgment	12-2-96
8. Plaintiff's Response to Defendants' Motion for Summary Judgment	12-2-96
9. Plaintiff's Motion to Strike Affidavit of Ralph Carter in Opposition to Plaintiff's Motion for Summary Judgment	12-2-96
10. Affidavit of Harry Edwards in Support of Plaintiff's First Amended Motion for Summary Judgment	12-12-96
11. Plaintiff's Response to Defendants' First Set of Interrogatories and Request for Production	1-13-97
12. Plaintiff's Motion to Strike Affidavit of Laura K. Summer	1-22-97
13. Plaintiff's Motion for Continuance	1-22-97

Index to Defendants' Pleadings

TITLE OF DOCUMENT	DATE FILED, RECEIVED OR DATE OF CERT. OF SERVICE
1. Defendants' Original Answer	6-9-96
2. Defendants' First Request for Admission of Facts	7-11-96
3. Defendants' First Original Counterclaim Petition	Rec. 9-9-96
4. Defendants' Motion for Summary Judgment	Rec. 9-28-96
5. Affidavit of Ralph Carter	Rec. 9-28-96
6. Defendants' First Amended Motion for Summary Judgment	Cert. 11-16-96
7. Defendants' Response to Plaintiff's Motion for Summary Judgment	Rec. 12-5-96
8. Defendants' Brief in Support of Motion for Summary Judgment	Cert. 12-5-96 Rec. 12-7-96
9. Defendants' First Set of Interrogatories and Request for Production	Cert. 12-15-96 Rec. 12-19-96
10. Affidavit of Laura K. Summer	Cert. 1-16-97

UNIT 7—EXERCISE 2

Cash Deposit in Lieu of Appeal Bond

CAUSE NO. C-36,848

WALLACE PARADISE CORPORATION	§	IN THE DISTRICT COURT
	§	
Plaintiff,	§	
	§	
vs.	§	
	§	
DALLAS CENTRAL APPRAISAL DISTRICT and APPRAISAL REVIEW BOARD OF DALLAS CENTRAL APPRAISAL DISTRICT,	§ § §	142nd JUDICIAL DISTRICT
	§	
Defendants.	§	DALLAS COUNTY, TEXAS

CASH DEPOSIT IN LIEU OF APPEAL BOND

WHEREAS, in the above-entitled and numbered cause pending in the 142nd Judicial District Court of Dallas County, Texas, and at a regular term thereof, on February 26, 19__, judgment was rendered in favor of Dallas Central Appraisal District and Appraisal Review Board of Dallas Central Appraisal District, Defendants, and against Wallace Paradise Corporation, Plaintiff, from which judgment Plaintiff desires to appeal to the Court of Appeals for the Fifth Supreme Judicial District of Texas;

NOW, THEREFORE, Wallace Paradise Corporation, as Plaintiff, acknowledges itself bound to deposit with the Clerk of the Court, the cash sum of $1,000 as prescribed by Rule 46 of the Rules of Appellate Procedure, conditioned that Appellant shall prosecute its appeal with effect, and shall pay all costs which have accrued in the trial court and the costs of the Statement of Facts and transcript.

WITNESS ITS HANDS this _________ day of March, 19__.

WALLACE PARADISE CORPORATION,

By: ____________________________________
Bruce McDonnell, President

(*Instruction:* Insert Certificate of Service.)

UNIT 7—EXERCISE 3

Request to Clerk to Include Material in Transcript

CAUSE NO. C-36,848

WALLACE PARADISE CORPORATION	§	IN THE DISTRICT COURT
	§	
Plaintiff,	§	
	§	
vs.	§	
	§	
DALLAS CENTRAL APPRAISAL DISTRICT and APPRAISAL REVIEW BOARD OF DALLAS CENTRAL APPRAISAL DISTRICT,	§	142nd JUDICIAL DISTRICT
	§	
	§	
	§	
Defendants.	§	DALLAS COUNTY, TEXAS

REQUEST TO CLERK TO INCLUDE MATERIAL IN TRANSCRIPT

TO THE CLERK OF SAID COURT:

Wallace Paradise Corporation, hereinafter referred to as "Appellant," who has deposited cash in lieu of bond in the above-referenced cause, requests the Clerk of the Court to prepare, for inclusion in the transcript of these proceedings, the following designated matters in addition to any other matters required by law or the Texas Rules of Appellate Procedure to be contained therein:

DOCUMENT TITLE	**FILING DATE**
Plaintiff's Original Petition	05-18-96
Order (depositing money into Registry of the Court)	05-18-96
Defendants' Original Answer	06-09-96
Defendants' First Request for Admission of Facts and Genuineness of Documents	07-11-96
Agreed Order Extending Time to Respond to Request for Admissions	08-22-96

Plaintiff's Answer to Defendants' First Request for Admission of Facts and Genuineness of Documents	09-01-96
Defendants' Motion for Summary Judgment	09-26-96
Affidavit in support of Motion for Summary Judgment (Carter)	09-26-96
Plaintiff's First Amended Original Petition	12-02-96
Defendants' Response to Plaintiff's Motion for Summary Judgment	12-02-96
Motion of Wallace Paradise Corporation to Strike the Summary Judgment Affidavit of Ralph Carter	12-02-96
Affidavit of Laura K. Summer	01-16-97
Plaintiff's Response to Motion to Dismiss for Lack of Jurisdiction and to Plea in Abatement for Lack of Venue	07-14-97
Orders Relative to Motions for Summary Judgment	02-26-98
Summary Judgment	02-26-98
Cash Deposit in Lieu of Appeal Bond	03-27-98
Clerk's Certificate of Cash Deposit in Lieu of Appeal Bond	03-27-98

All other matters required by law or rules of procedure to be included in the transcript.

Respectfully submitted,

Signature Block

ATTORNEY FOR APPELLANT

(*Instructions:* Insert Certificate of Service.)

UNIT 7—EXERCISE 4

Title Page for Court of Appeals

No. 05-90-00104-CV

IN THE COURT OF APPEALS

5TH DISTRICT OF TEXAS

DALLAS, TEXAS

WALLACE PARADISE CORPORATION,

Appellant,

V.

DALLAS CENTRAL APPRAISAL DISTRICT and
APPRAISAL REVIEW BOARD OF DALLAS
CENTRAL APPRAISAL DISTRICT,

Appellees.

ON APPEAL FROM THE 142ND JUDICIAL DISTRICT

COURT OF DALLAS COUNTY, TEXAS

BRIEF OF APPELLANT, WALLACE PARADISE CORPORATION

Signature Block

ATTORNEY FOR APPELLANT

UNIT 7—EXERCISE 5

Index of Authorities

UNIT 8

Family Law

Although family law includes laws relative to individuals within a relationship—that is, marriage, divorce, child custody, adoption, and so on—the terms presented in this unit primarily concern marriage and divorce. Whereas civil litigation is adversarial (one side against the other), there is growing interest in making all areas of family law nonadversarial, as evidenced by the no-fault divorce laws adopted in many states.

VOCABULARY

adoption
(ə-dŏp′-shən) — The legal taking of another's child and giving the child all of the rights, privileges, and duties of a natural child.

alimony pendente lite
(ăl′-ə-mō-nē pĕn-dĕn′-tē lī′-tē) — Money paid to a spouse for support while a divorce action is pending.

annulment
(ə-nŭl′-mənt) — The voiding of a marriage and treating it as if it never existed.

antenuptial agreement
(ăn-tə-nŭp′-shəl ə-grē′-mənt) — An agreement made between two people before they marry; also called a premarital agreement.

cohabitation
(kō-hăb′-ĭ-tā′-shən) — Living together as husband and wife.

common-law marriage
(kŏm′-ən--lô măr′-ĭj*) — A marriage existing between two people who agree to live as husband and wife without legal ceremony.

community property
(kə-myōō′-nə-tē prŏp′-ər-tē) — In some states, property acquired by husband and wife during marriage and considered the property of both parties.

corespondent
(kō-rĭ-spŏn′-dənt) — A party charged with committing adultery with the respondent in a divorce action.

*The double hyphen (--) indicates a hyphen in the word as opposed to a division between syllables.

custody (kŭs′-tə-dē)	The care and possession of minor children of a marriage during a divorce proceeding and after divorce is final.
desertion (dĭ-zûr′-shən)	The refusal without cause of a husband or wife to continue a marital relationship.
divorce (dĭ-vôrs′)	Legal dissolution of a marriage.
irreconcilable (ĭ-rĕk-ən-sī′-lə-bəl)	Positions so different that it is impossible to bring the opposing views together; incapable of compromise.
petitioner (pə-tĭsh′-ən-ər)	Another word for plaintiff; often used in family law.
privileged communications (prĭv′-ə-lĭjd kə-myōō-nə-kā′-shəns)	Certain oral or written communications of a party that cannot be admitted into evidence; for example, between attorney and client, between husband and wife.
respondent (rĭ-spŏn′-dənt)	Another word for defendant, used in many family law cases.
separate maintenance (sĕp′-ə-rāt mān′-tə-nəns)	The amount granted to one spouse by a court in a legal separation for his or her support and the support of the children.
separate property (sĕp′-ə-rāt prŏp′-ər-tē)	Property owned by either spouse before marriage or acquired during marriage by gift or inheritance.
separation (sĕp-ə-rā′-shən)	A situation in which parties are not living together but otherwise have legal duties of husband and wife.
valid marriage (văl′-ĭd măr′-ĭj)	A marriage created according to the legal requirements.
void marriage (void măr′-ĭj)	A marriage that does not meet the legal requirements of a valid marriage; it cannot be valid under any circumstances.
voidable marriage (voi′-də-bəl măr′-ĭj)	A marriage that exists for all practical purposes but could be declared void in a court of law.

VOCABULARY-DICTATION

Living together as husband and wife, either married or unmarried, is termed <u>cohabitation</u>. Under the laws of some states, <u>common-law marriage</u> may exist between two people who agree to live as husband and wife without legal ceremony.

An <u>antenuptial agreement</u> is an agreement made between two people before they marry; it is also called a premarital agreement. This is generally related to property rights. Property owned by either spouse before marriage or acquired during marriage by gift or inheritance is <u>separate property</u>. In some states, property acquired by a husband and wife during marriage is <u>community property</u> and belongs to the parties jointly.

Under the law concerning <u>privileged communications</u>, a spouse is not required nor allowed to testify against the other spouse regarding information that is known as a result of the marital relationship.

Under certain circumstances, an annulment may be granted which voids a marriage and treats it as if it never existed. A valid marriage is one created according to the legal requirements. A void marriage is one that does not meet the legal requirements of a valid marriage; it cannot be valid under any circumstances (e.g., if one party is already married). A voidable marriage is one that exists for all practical purposes but that could, under certain circumstances, be declared void in a court of law.

Legally speaking, separation, as opposed to divorce, is a situation in which parties are not living together but otherwise have the legal duties of husband and wife. Separate maintenance is the amount granted to one spouse by the court in a legal separation for his or her support and the support of the children.

Divorce is the legal dissolution of a marriage. Alimony pendente lite is money paid on a temporary basis to a spouse for support while the divorce action is pending. The care and possession of minor children of a marriage during a divorce proceeding and after divorce is final is termed custody. An adoption is the legal taking of another's child and giving the child all of the rights, privileges, and duties of a natural child.

In states with no-fault divorce laws, the statutes try to avoid adversary terminology. Instead of *plaintiff,* the term petitioner is used in many family law cases. Instead of *defendant,* the party sued is referred to as the respondent. Among the grounds for divorce is desertion, which is the refusal without cause of a husband or wife to continue a marital relationship. When the parties have views so different that there is no possibility of compromise, the grounds for divorce are expressed as irreconcilable differences. An individual charged with committing adultery with the respondent in a divorce action is referred to as the corespondent.

SELF-TEST—UNIT 8

1. One of the grounds for divorce is ______________________, which is the refusal without cause of a husband or wife to continue a marital relationship.

2. Under the law concerning ______________________, a spouse is not required nor allowed to testify against the other spouse regarding information that is known as a result of the marital relationship.

3. Under the laws of some states, if two people agree to live as husband and wife without legal ceremony, they are said to have a(n) ___________ ___________.

4. Under certain circumstances, a(n) _______________ may be granted, which voids a marriage and treats it as if it never existed.
5. A(n) _______________ is one that does not meet legal requirements of a valid marriage; it cannot be valid under any circumstances (e.g., if one party is already married).
6. The care and possession of minor children of a marriage during divorce proceeding and after divorce is final is termed _______________.
7. A(n) _______________ is one that exists for all practical purposes but that could be declared void in a court of law.
8. The most common recited ground for divorce is _______________ differences, wherein the parties' differences are so great that it is impossible to bring the opposing views together.
9. _______________ is the amount granted to one spouse by the court in a legal separation for his or her support and the support of the children.
10. In some states, property acquired and jointly owned by a husband and wife during marriage is referred to as _______________.
11. _______________ is the legal dissolution of a marriage.
12. A(n) _______________ is one created according to the legal requirements.
13. _______________ is money paid on a temporary basis to the husband or wife as support while the divorce action is pending.
14. Property owned by either spouse before marriage or acquired during marriage by gift or inheritance is _______________.
15. Instead of *plaintiff,* the term _______________ is used in many family law cases.

16. A(n) ________________________ is an agreement made between two people before they marry; it is also called a premarital agreement.
17. An individual charged with committing adultery with the respondent in a divorce action is referred to as the ________________________.
18. Legally speaking, ________________________, as opposed to divorce, is a situation in which parties are not living together but otherwise have the legal duties of husband and wife.
19. Instead of the designation *defendant,* the party being sued in a family law case may be referred to as the ________________________.
20. Living together as husband and wife is termed ________________________.
21. A(n) ________________________ is the legal taking of another's child and giving the child all of the rights, privileges, and duties of a natural child.

UNIT 8—EXERCISE 1

Prenuptial Agreement

PRENUPTIAL AGREEMENT

Bruce Roberts, of Dallas, Dallas County, Texas, and Wanda L. Daniels, of Richardson, Dallas County, Texas, contemplate their future marriage on or about December 7, 19__, and in consideration of such future marriage, the parties have entered into an agreement with respect to such marriage for the following reasons and with reference to the following facts:

ARTICLE I.

Sec. 1.1 Purpose. The parties to this agreement intend and desire to define that property that each party brings to the marriage, to the end that such property will be designated and set apart as the separate property of the respective parties. The parties wish to avoid the community property interests that, but for the operation of this agreement, they might have acquired in the property of the other as incidents of their marriage relationship. The parties further desire to set forth methods by which their respective community and separate property interest may be determined in the event the marriage is terminated by death or dissolution of the marriage or otherwise.

The parties to this agreement further desire to define the contributions that each party will make to the improvement and maintenance of the household from his or her separate property.

ARTICLE II.

Sec. 2.1 Disclosure of Property. Both parties to this agreement have made to each other a full and complete disclosure of the nature, extent, and probable value of all of their real and personal property, and tangible and intangible assets. Such disclosure has been made verbally and by a written document furnished to each party, and each party hereto acknowledges having received the same.

Sec. 2.2 Agreement Conditioned on Marriage. The parties enter into this agreement in consideration of marriage. The effectiveness of this agreement is expressly conditioned on the occurrence of such marriage. If for any reason the marriage does not take place, the agreement will be of no force or effect.

Sec. 2.3 Representation by Independent Counsel. Wanda L. Daniels admits and acknowledges that each party has been represented by independent legal counsel in the negotiation of this agreement. Wanda L. Daniels further acknowledges that she freely chose ______________________________ to act as her own legal counsel, that she has read this agreement, and that her counsel has explained to her the legal meaning and consequences of the agreement.

Bruce Roberts admits and acknowledges that each party has been represented by independent legal counsel in the negotiation of this agreement. Bruce Roberts further acknowledges that he freely chose Michelle L. Underwood to act as his own legal counsel, that he has read this agreement, and that his counsel has explained to him the legal meaning and consequences of the agreement.

ARTICLE III.

Sec. 3.1 Property Management. Wanda L. Daniels will have sole and exclusive management of her separate property. Bruce Roberts will have sole and exclusive management of his separate property. Each party reserves the right to make gifts of his or her separate property and reserves the right to sell, mortgage, or otherwise deal with his or her separate property without consulting the non-managing spouse.

Sec. 3.2 Property Income. As permitted by Article 16, Section 15, of the Texas Constitution, the parties agree that all of the income or property from all of the separate property of Wanda L. Daniels will be her separate property.

As permitted by Article 16, Section 15, of the Texas Constitution, the parties agree that all the income or property from all of the separate property of Bruce Roberts will be his separate property.

This provision applies both to the separate property the parties owned prior to the marriage and to the separate property that may be acquired during the marriage.

Sec. 3.3 Other Provisions Regarding Separate Property. Any recovery for personal injuries sustained by a spouse during the marriage, except any recovery for loss of earning capacity during marriage, will be the separate property of the spouse suffering the personal injuries.

The following property will remain the separate property of the party who owns the original separate property:

(a) Property that is traceable to separate property owned before marriage;

(b) Property that is acquired during the marriage from separate funds;

(c) Property that is exchanged for separate property; and

(d) Property that is purchased with proceeds of sale of separate property.

Sec. 3.4 Agreement Regarding Future Earnings. As permitted by Article 16, Section 15, of the Texas Constitution, the parties agree to partition any future income from personal earnings as follows:

(a) All the earnings from personal services of Wanda L. Daniels will be the separate property of Wanda L. Daniels; and,

(b) All the earnings of Bruce Roberts from personal services will be community income.

Sec. 3.5 Payments and Improvements on Separate Property. The parties agree that if either party uses his or her own separate funds to make any payment toward the purchase of the other party's separate property, or either party uses community funds to make a payment toward the purchase of the separate property of the other party, the property so paid for will remain entirely the separate property of the owner-spouse. The party making such payment using his or her separate property will be entitled to reimbursement from the owner-spouse's separate property in the amount of the payment.

The parties agree that if either party uses his or her own separate funds to make any improvements on the other party's separate property, or either party uses community funds to make any improvement of the separate property of the other party, the property so improved will remain entirely the separate property of the owner-spouse. The party making such improvements using his or her separate property will be entitled to reimbursement as follows: either the cost of the improvements or the enhanced value of the separate property, whichever is less. If either party uses community funds to make such improvements, the community will be entitled to reimbursement in an amount to be measured as follows: either the cost of the improvements or the enhanced value of the separate property, whichever is less.

ARTICLE IV.

Sec. 4.1 Agreement to Join in Execution of Other Instruments. Both parties to this agreement covenant and agree that they will willingly, at the request of the other party, or at the request of his or her successors or assigns, execute, deliver, and properly acknowledge whatever additional instruments may be required to carry out the intention of this agreement, and will execute, deliver, and properly acknowledge any deeds or other documents necessary to effectuate this agreement.

Sec 4.2 Invalid Provisions. The parties agree that if any portion of this agreement is held invalid for any reason, the remainder of the agreement will remain in full force and effect.

Sec. 4.3 Term of Agreement. This agreement will terminate when the marriage terminates, whether by divorce, annulment, or death. The parties reserve the right to terminate this agreement by mutual, written agreement.

Sec. 4.4 Binding Effect. This agreement will bind and inure to the benefit of the respective heirs, personal representatives, successors, and assigns of the parties.

Sec. 4.5 Entire Agreement; Modification. This agreement contains the entire agreement between the parties. Any oral representations or modifications made before or after the execution of this agreement will be of no force or effect; provided, however, that this agreement may be altered or amended in the future by written agreement of the parties. Such written agreement must specifically refer to this agreement.

Sec. 4.6 Venue. The parties agree that venue for enforcement of this agreement will be in Dallas County, Texas.

We, Wanda L. Daniels and Bruce Roberts, in consideration of the premises, have signed our names to each of the foregoing pages of this agreement, consisting of ______________ (_____) pages including the page containing our acknowledgement on this the ________ day of October, 19__.

______________________________ ______________________________

Wanda L. Daniels Bruce Roberts

STATE OF TEXAS §
§
COUNTY OF DALLAS §

This instrument was acknowledged before me on the ______ day of October, 19__ by Wanda L. Daniels and Bruce Roberts.

____

Notary Public, State of Texas

My Commission Expires:

____

CERTIFICATION OF ATTORNEY FOR WANDA L. DANIELS

I certify that I am an attorney at law, duly licensed and admitted to practice in the State of Texas; that I have been employed by Wanda L. Daniels, a party to this agreement, and that I have advised her with respect to this contract and explained to her its meaning and legal effects, and that Wanda L. Daniels has acknowledged a full and complete understanding of this agreement and its legal consequences, and has freely and voluntarily executed the agreement in my presence.

Signed this ________ day of October, 19__.

____
Attorney for Wanda L. Daniels

CERTIFICATION OF ATTORNEY FOR BRUCE ROBERTS

I certify that I am an attorney at law, duly licensed and admitted to practice in the State of Texas; that I have been employed by Bruce Roberts, a party to this agreement, and that I have advised him with respect to this contract and explained to him its meaning and legal effects, and that Bruce Roberts has acknowledged a full and complete understanding of this agreement and its legal consequences, and has freely and voluntarily executed the agreement in my presence.

Signed this __________ day of October, 19__.

____
Michelle L. Underwood,
Attorney for Bruce Roberts

UNIT 8—EXERCISE 2

Divorce Petition

CAUSE NO. ____________________

IN THE MATTER OF THE MARRIAGE OF	§	IN THE DISTRICT COURT
SALLY SUE LAWRENCE,	§	
	§	
Petitioner,	§	______ JUDICIAL DISTRICT
	§	
AND	§	
	§	
BILLY BOB LAWRENCE,	§	
	§	
Respondent.	§	DALLAS COUNTY, TEXAS

ORIGINAL PETITION

This suit is brought by Sally Sue Lawrence, Petitioner, age 39, who resides at 3414 Lightning Rod Road, Dallas, Texas 75230.

Respondent is Billy Bob Lawrence, age 39, who resides at 2614 Hill Street, Dallas, Texas 75238.

I. RESIDENCY

Petitioner has been a domiciliary of the State of Texas for the preceding six (6) months and a resident of the county in which this petition is filed for the preceding ninety (90) days.

II. SERVICE OF PROCESS

Waiver: No service is necessary at this time.

III. MARRIAGE

Petitioner and Respondent were married on or about February 14, 1982 and lived together as husband and wife until on or about August 6, 19__, at which time they separated and ceased to live together.

IV. GROUNDS

The marriage has become insupportable because of discord and conflict and personalities that destroy the legitimate ends of the marriage relationship and prevent any reasonable expectation of reconciliation.

V. PROPERTY

No property: To Petitioner's knowledge, there is no community property of any significant value other than personal effects which is subject to division by the Court at this time.

There has been no child born to this marriage nor is any expected.

No other person is entitled to notice of this suit.

PRAYER

Petitioner prays that citation and notice issue as required by law and that the Court grant a divorce and decree such other relief as is requested in this petition.

Petitioner prays for such other and further relief, general and special, to which Petitioner may be entitled.

DATED ____________________________________, 19_____.

______________________________,
Petitioner, In Pro Per
Address:
3414 Lightning Rod Road
Dallas, Texas 75230

UNIT 8—EXERCISE 3

Waiver of Citation

NO. 89-17091-J

IN THE MATTER OF THE MARRIAGE	§	IN THE DISTRICT COURT
OF SALLY SUE LAWRENCE,	§	
	§	
Petitioner,	§	_______ JUDICIAL DISTRICT
	§	
AND	§	
	§	
BILLY BOB LAWRENCE,	§	
	§	
Respondent.	§	DALLAS COUNTY, TEXAS

WAIVER OF CITATION

STATE OF TEXAS §
§
COUNTY OF DALLAS §

Before me, the undersigned authority, on this day personally appeared BILLY BOB LAWRENCE, who, being duly sworn, upon his oath states:

"I, BILLY BOB LAWRENCE, am the Respondent in the above-entitled and numbered cause. My mailing address is 2614 Hill Street, Dallas, Texas 75238. I have been given a copy of the Original Petition for Divorce that has been filed in this cause, and I have read it and understand it. I have further been given a copy of the proposed Decree of Divorce and approved same. I hereby enter my appearance in this cause for all purposes and waive the issuance and service of citation upon me. I agree that the petition may be amended and that the cause may be taken up and considered by the Court without further notice to me. I waive the making of a record of testimony.

"Further, I hereby waive all rights and privileges, including appointment of counsel, pursuant of the Soldiers and Sailors Civil Relief Act of 1940."

____

BILLY BOB LAWRENCE

SUBSCRIBED AND SWORN TO before me this __________ day of ________________, 19____.

____

Notary Public, State of Texas

UNIT 9

Probate

Section 9A
Testamentary Wills

In common usage, the word *Will,* by itself, is used to indicate a document that disposes of one's property. In the legal field, in order to be precise, such a document is entitled "Last Will and Testament." This title encompasses both one's wishes or desires (Will) and the disposition of property to occur after death (Testament or Testamentary).

VOCABULARY

attestation clause (ăt-ĕs-tā′shən klôz)	A written statement by witnesses to the signing of a document by the testator.
codicil (kŏd′ə-sĭl)	An addition to a will that modifies or changes it in some way.
estate (ĕ-stāt′)	The real and personal property of the testator.
holographic will (hŏl′ə-grăf-ĭk wĭl)	A will that is entirely handwritten by the testator.
intestate (ĭn-tĕs′tāt)	One who dies without having made a will.
nuncupative will (nŭng′kyə-pā-tĭv wĭl)	An oral will, usually made in anticipation of immediate death.
per stirpes (pûr stĕr′pēz)	Children of one heir of the testator may take only the portion of the estate that the parent would have taken if living.
residue (rĕz′ə-do͞o)	That part of an estate remaining after debts, taxes, and special bequests.
testamentary capacity (tĕs′tə-mĕn-tə-rē kə-păs′ə-tē)	The mental capacity required by law to be sufficient to make a will.
testator (tĕs′tā-tər)	A person (male) who makes a will.

testatrix (tĕs-tā′-trĭks)	A person (female) who makes a will.
testimonium clause (tĕs-tĭ-mō′-nē-əm klôz)	Last clause in a will preceding the testator's signature; relates to date and circumstances of execution by testator.
will (wĭl)	A legal document that expresses the testator's wishes regarding his estate.

VOCABULARY-DICTATION

An individual's estate includes all of his property, both real and personal. If a person dies without having made a will, he is said to have died intestate.

A will, formally called "Last Will and Testament," is a legal document that expresses the testator's wishes regarding his estate. The degree of mental capacity required by law to be sufficient to make a will is referred to as testamentary capacity. The person making the will is called either the testator (male) or the testatrix (female). In some states, the word "testator" is used to designate both men and women, but in Texas the masculine and feminine versions are generally used.

Bequests to the testator's children are often followed, in the will, by the Latin phrase per stirpes, which means the children of that heir may take only the portion of the estate the parent would have taken if living. The part of an estate remaining after debts, taxes, and special bequests is the residue.

A holographic will is one that is entirely handwritten by the testator. An oral will, usually made in anticipation of immediate death, is called a nuncupative will. The last clause in a will before the testator's signature is the testimonium clause, which relates to date and circumstances of execution by testator. The attestation clause, often referred to as the *self-proving clause,* is a written statement signed by the witnesses confirming the signing of the document by the testator.

A codicil is an addition to a will that modifies or changes it in some way. A codicil is usually written some time after the execution of the will and reflects some change(s) in the testator's wishes.

SELF-TEST—UNIT 9A

1. The ________________________ is the last clause in a will before the testator's signature.

2. If a person dies without having made a will, he is said to have died ________________________.

3. A(n) ________________________ is one that is entirely handwritten by the testator.

4. The degree of mental capacity required by law to be sufficient to make a will is referred to as ______________________.

5. An individual's ______________________ includes all of his property, both real and personal.

6. The person making the will is called either the ______________________ (male) or the ______________________ (female).

7. A(n) ______________________ is an addition to a will that modifies or changes it in some way.

8. ______________________ is a Latin phrase that means that the children of an heir may take only the portion of the estate the parent would have taken if living.

9. An oral will, usually made in anticipation of immediate death, is called a ______________________.

10. A(n) ______________________ is a legal document that expresses the testator's wishes regarding his estate.

11. The ______________________, often referred to as the *self-proving clause,* is a written statement signed by the witnesses confirming the signing of the document by the testator.

12. The part of an estate remaining after debts, taxes, and special bequests is the ______________________.

UNIT 9A - EXERCISE 1

Last Will and Testament

LAST WILL AND TESTAMENT OF JOAN COLFAX

STATE OF TEXAS	§	
	§	KNOW ALL MEN BY THESE PRESENTS:
COUNTY OF DALLAS	§	

That I, JOAN COLFAX, a resident of Dallas County, State of Texas, being in good health, of sound and disposing mind and memory and above the age of eighteen (18) years, do hereby make and publish this my Last Will and Testament, hereby revoking all wills made by me heretofore at any time.

ARTICLE ONE

I do hereby nominate, constitute, and appoint my daughter, PAULA COLFAX BOYD, Independent Executrix of this my Will; provided, however, that in the event she be not living or be or become incapable of acting, then or in either of such events, I hereby appoint my daughter, JANE COLFAX, Independent Executrix and as Successor Independent Executrix of this my Will, and direct that no bond shall be required of either of them, and that no other action shall be had in the Probate Court in regard to the settlement of my estate than the probating and recording of this my Last Will and Testament and the return of the statutory inventory, appraisement, and list of claims of said estate. Subject to the specific bequests set forth in ARTICLE THREE, I do hereby authorize and empower my said Executrix and Successor Executrix, if any, to sell, dispose of, deliver and convey any portion of my estate, real or personal, at private or public sale, for any price and on any terms, and in any manner that seems to said Executrix or Successor Executrix, if any, best for any purpose. The Executrix or Successor Executrix, if any, of my estate shall have the power to satisfy any devise hereunder wholly in cash, or in kind, or as undivided interests, or in any combination thereof, and the determination of values hereof made by said Executrix or Successor Executrix, if any, under this Will shall be conclusive on all beneficiaries under this my Last Will and Testament.

ARTICLE TWO

I hereby authorize and empower my Independent Executrix and Successor Executrix, if any, to pay all of my debts, expenses of last illness and funeral, all other proper charges against my estate, expenses of administration and all federal and state estate or inheritance taxes, if any, payable at the time of my death out of my residuary estate without apportionment and without right of contribution by any recipient of any properties passing by reason of my death; provided, however, the Executrix and Successor Executrix, if any, of my estate will not sell, encumber, or dispose of the items of personalty constituting the specific bequests described in ARTICLE FOUR for any purpose under the provisions of this ARTICLE TWO; it being my intention that such personalty shall be distributed under the terms of the specific bequest in ARTICLE FOUR. I hereby waive on behalf of my estate any right to recover any part of such taxes, interest or penalties from any person, including any beneficiary of insurance on my life and anyone who may have received from me or from my estate any property which is taxable as a part of my estate.

ARTICLE THREE

After the payment of my debts, funeral expenses, and expenses of my last illness, I will, give, bequeath and devise all of my property, both real and personal, or mixed, wheresoever situated and howsoever acquired, I may die seized and possessed of, or have any interest in, to my beloved husband, JAMES COLFAX, in fee simple absolute.

ARTICLE FOUR

I give and bequeath to my son, MICHAEL COLFAX, two gold men's rings. I give and bequeath one lady's diamond ring to my daughter, PAULA COLFAX BOYD, and one lady's sapphire ring to my daughter, JANE COLFAX.

In the event any legatee named above in this ARTICLE FOUR shall predecease me and be not living at the date of my death, then in that event, such special bequest to such beneficiary shall lapse and pass to and become a part of my residuary estate.

ARTICLE FIVE

In the event my said husband, JAMES COLFAX, does not survive me, or dies simultaneously with me, or in a common disaster, then I will, give, bequeath and devise my estate, both real and personal, or mixed, separate or community, and wherever situated to my children, PAULA COLFAX BOYD, JANE COLFAX, and MICHAEL COLFAX, per stirpes, share and share alike.

ARTICLE SIX

Any share or portion of a share of any trust created hereunder, or any other property of mine that is not disposed of under any other provision of this Will, shall pass and be distributed to my heirs-at-law. Their identity and respective shares shall be determined in all respects as if my death had occurred immediately following the happening of the event requiring such distribution, and according to the laws of the State of Texas then in force governing the distribution of separate, personal property of an intestate.

ARTICLE SEVEN

No interest of any beneficiary in the corpus or income of my estate or of any trust created hereunder shall be subject to assignment, alienation, pledge, attachment or claims of creditors of such beneficiary, and no such interest may otherwise be voluntarily or involuntarily alienated or encumbered by such beneficiary, except as may be otherwise expressly provided herein.

ARTICLE EIGHT

Any property subject to any mortgage, lien, or other encumbrance bequeathed or devised hereunder, either outright or in trust, shall pass and be distributed subject to such mortgage, lien, or other encumbrance.

ARTICLE NINE

If any provision of this Will shall be unenforceable, the remaining provisions shall nevertheless be carried into effect.

IN TESTIMONY WHEREOF, I hereunto sign my name and for verification I have also signed my name on each of the foregoing pages of this my Last Will and Testament, consisting of _____ pages including attestation and self-proving provision, in the presence of the undersigned witnesses who signed their names hereto as witnesses at my request, in my presence, and in the presence of each other this _________ day of ________________, 19____.

____
JOAN COLFAX

On this date JOAN COLFAX declared to us that this instrument was her Will, and she requested each of us to act as witnesses to it and to her signature on it. She then signed the Will in the presence of all of us. We now at her request, in her presence and in the presence of each other, sign our names as witnesses to her Will and each of us declares that in his or her opinion the Testatrix is of sound mind.

____
WITNESS

____
ADDRESS

____

____
WITNESS

____
ADDRESS

____

STATE OF TEXAS §
§
COUNTY OF DALLAS §

BEFORE ME, the undersigned authority, on this day personally appeared JOAN COLFAX, ____________________ and ____________________, known to me to be the Testatrix and the Witnesses, respectively, whose names are subscribed to the annexed or foregoing instrument in their respective capacities. All of these persons being duly sworn by me, JOAN COLFAX, the Testatrix, declared to me and to the Witnesses in my presence that this instrument is her Will and she had willingly made and executed it as her free act and deed for the purposes expressed in it. The Witnesses, each under oath, stated to me in the presence and hearing of the Testatrix that the Testatrix declared to them that this instrument is her Will and that she executed it as such and wanted each of them to sign it as a witness. The Witnesses also stated under oath that they signed the instrument as witnesses in the presence of the Testatrix at her request, that the Testatrix was at that time at least eighteen (18) years of age and was of sound mind and that each of the witnesses was at that time at least fourteen (14) years of age.

____
JOAN COLFAX, Testatrix

____
Witness

____
Witness

SUBSCRIBED AND ACKNOWLEDGED BEFORE ME by the said JOAN COLFAX, Testatrix, and SUBSCRIBED AND SWORN TO BEFORE ME by the said ____________________ and ____________________, witnesses, this __________ day of ________________, 19____.

____
Notary Public, The State of Texas

My Commission Expires:

____
Printed Name of Notary

____

Section 9B
Wills and Probate

Strictly interpreted, *Probate* is the judgment that an instrument is a valid will. The term is commonly used to include all aspects of settling a decedent's estate. The second section of this unit contains additional terms relative to wills as well as terms applicable to the probate of a will.

VOCABULARY

administrator (ād-mĭn-ĭs-trā′-tōr)	A person (male) appointed by the Court to carry out the probate of an estate in the absence of a will.
administrator cum testamento annexo (ād-mĭn-ĭs-trā′-tōr kūm tĕs-tă-mĕn′-tō ăn-nĕ′-xō)	A person (male) appointed by the Court to administer a will in the event the executor is unable or unwilling to do so.
administratrix (ād-mĭn-ĭs-trā′-trĭks)	A person (female) appointed by the Court to carry out the probate of an estate in the absence of a will.
beneficiary (bĕn-ə-fĭsh′-ē-ĕr-ē)	Anyone who benefits under the terms of a will.
bequeath (bĭ-kwēth′)	To give something, usually personal property, under terms of a will.
bequest (bĭ-kwĕst′)	Something, usually personal property, given under terms of a will.
chattel (chăt′l)	Personal property; does not include real property.
conservator (kən-sûr-və-tər)	A person appointed to manage and/or care for the property of a minor or an incompetent.
devise (dĭ-vīz′)	To give real property to another under the terms of a will.

escheat (ĕs-chēt′)	The reversion of all the property of an estate to the state when there are no competent heirs.
executor (ĕg-zĕk′-yə-tər)	A person (male) designated in a will to carry out testator's wishes.
executrix (ĕg-zĕk′-yə-trĭks)	A person (female) designated in a will to carry out testator's wishes.
guardian (gär′-dē-ən)	A person legally responsible for the care of a minor and/or the minor's estate.
guardian ad litem (gär′-dē-ən ăd lī′-tĕm)	Latin; a person designated by the court to conduct litigation on behalf of a minor or an incompetent.
heir (âr)	Anyone who has a legal right to inherit the property of another.
hereditament (hĕr-ə-dĭt′-ə-mənt)	Any kind of property, real or personal, that may be inherited.
muniment of title (myōō′-nə-mənt ŭv tīt′l)	A document evidencing title.
precatory words (prĕk′-ə-tôr-ē wûrds)	A part of a will that expresses the testator's desire but is not binding on the court.
probate (prō′-bāt)	The official proving of a will to be valid.
residuary estate (rĭ-zĭj′-ōō-ĕr-ē ĕ-stāt′)	The estate remaining after debts, expenses, and specific bequests have been settled.
trust (trŭst)	Property placed in the care of one person for the benefit of another.
ward (wôrd)	A person who has a legal guardian.

VOCABULARY-DICTATION

Probate is the official proving of a will to be valid. An executor (male) or executrix (female) is the person designated in a will to carry out the wishes of the testator. If an individual dies intestate, the court may appoint an administrator (male) or an administratrix (female) to administer the estate. An administrator cum testamento annexo (male) is appointed by the court to administer a will in the event the executor is unable or unwilling to do so. Precatory words constitute that part of a will that expresses the testator's desire but is not binding on the court.

The verb devise means to give real property to another under the terms of a will. Some type of written document is required to transfer title to real property from one person to another. A muniment of title is an original document that serves this purpose. The verb bequeath means to give something, usually personal property, under the terms of a will. A bequest (noun) is usually personal property (may range from a plastic flower to a 10-carat diamond) given under the terms of a will. A person's chattels refers to personal property; real property is not included. The word hereditament covers any kind of property, real or personal, that may be inherited. The estate remaining after all debts, expenses, and specific bequests have been settled is called the <u>residuary estate</u>. <u>Escheat</u> is the reversion of all the property of an estate to the state when there are no competent heirs.

Property placed in the care of one person for the benefit of another is said to be a <u>trust</u>. A <u>ward</u> is any person who has a legal guardian. The <u>guardian</u> is the person legally responsible for the care of a minor and/or the minor's estate. A Latin phrase, <u>guardian ad litem</u>, means a person designated by the court to conduct litigation on behalf of a minor or an incompetent. A person appointed to manage and/or care for the property, but not the person, of a minor or an incompetent is referred to as a <u>conservator</u>.

An <u>heir</u> is anyone who has a legal right to inherit the property of another; however, this does not necessarily mean he will inherit. On the other hand, a <u>beneficiary</u> is one who actually inherits or benefits under the terms of a will.

SELF-TEST—UNIT 9B

1. ______________________ are only personal property; real property is not included.
2. A(n) ______________________ (male) or ______________________ (female) is the person designated in a will to carry out the wishes of the testator.
3. A(n) ______________________ is appointed by the Court to administer a will in the event the executor is unable or unwilling to do so.
4. The estate remaining after all debts, expenses, and specific bequests have been settled is called the ______________________.
5. ______________________ constitute that part of a will that expresses the testator's desire but is not binding on the court.
6. To transfer title to real property from a decedent to an heir, the probate court may order a(n) ______________________.
7. A person appointed to manage and/or care for the property, but not the person, of a minor or an incompetent is referred to as a(n) ______________________.
8. To ______________________ means to give something, usually personal property, under the terms of a will.

9. ________________________ is the official proving of a will to be valid.

10. A(n) ________________________ is usually personal property given under the terms of a will.

11. ________________________ is any kind of property, real or personal, that may be inherited.

12. If a person dies intestate, the Court may appoint a(n) ____________ ____________ (male) or a(n) ________________________ (female) to administer the estate.

13. ________________________ is the reversion of all the property of an estate to the state when there are no competent heirs.

14. The ________________________ is the person legally responsible for the care of a minor and/or the minor's estate.

15. Anyone who benefits under the terms of a will is a(n) ____________ ____________.

16. The verb ________________________ means to give real property to another under the terms of a will.

17. Property placed in the care of one person for the benefit of another is said to be a(n) ________________________.

18. ________________________ refers to a person designated by the court to conduct litigation on behalf of a minor or an incompetent.

19. A(n) ________________________ is anyone who has a legal right to inherit the property of another.

20. A(n) ________________________ is any person who has a legal guardian.

UNIT 9B—EXERCISE 1

Application to Probate Will

NO. ____________________

IN THE MATTER OF	§	IN THE COUNTY COURT
	§	
THE ESTATE OF	§	OF
	§	
ROSE HARRIS, DECEASED	§	DALLAS COUNTY, TEXAS

APPLICATION TO PROBATE WILL

TO SAID HONORABLE COURT:

NOW COMES Norma Jean Harris, a person interested in the above referenced estate, and would show the Court as follows:

I.

Applicant, Norma Jean Harris, resides at 1505 Stephens Street, Dallas, Texas.

II.

Rose Harris died on the 25th day of February, 19__, in Dallas, Dallas County, Texas, at which time she was sixty (60) years of age and domiciled at 141 SW Browning, Dallas, Texas.

III.

This Court has jurisdiction and venue under the laws of the State of Texas for the reason that the Decedent had her domicile and fixed place of residence at and prior to her death within the County of Dallas, State of Texas, in which County and State her principal estate was located at the time of her death.

IV.

The principal portion of the Decedent's estate is located within Dallas County, Texas, and the total value of the real and personal property owned by the Decedent was in excess of Five Thousand and No/100 Dollars ($5,000.00).

V.

The Decedent left a written Will, duly executed on the 5th day of December, 1970, which is filed herewith; and in said Will the Applicant, Norma Jean Harris, was named Independent Executrix of said Will and estate, without bond, and without further action in the County Court other than the statutory return of inventory and appraisement of said estate. The names and addresses of the subscribing witnesses are as follows:

John Elliott, Dallas, Texas

Lee Russell, Dallas, Texas

VI.

That no child or children were born to or adopted by Decedent after the making of said Will by Decedent.

VII.

Applicant, Norma Jean Harris, was appointed and nominated by the Decedent as Independent Executrix of said Last Will and of said estate, and she is fully capable of acting as such Independent Executrix and is not disqualified by law from accepting Letters Testamentary.

VIII.

That Decedent was never divorced.

IX.

The social security number of the Applicant, Norma Jean Harris, is 466-44-9798, and the social security number of the Decedent, Rose Harris, is 436-32-3198.

X.

Applicant would further show that there exist no debts against said estate, and that there is no necessity for administration upon said estate, and that four (4) years have not elapsed since the death of the above-named Decedent and prior to this application.

WHEREFORE, Applicant prays that citation be issued herein as required by law and that upon hearing hereof the Will of Rose Harris, deceased, executed and dated on the 5th day of December, 1970, be admitted to probate as a Muniment of Title, and for such other orders and relief as to the Court may seem proper.

EXECUTED this __________ day of ________________, 19____.

____

(Signature Block)

ATTORNEY FOR APPLICANT

UNIT 9B—EXERCISE 2

Order Probating Will

NO. 90-39582

IN THE MATTER OF	§	IN THE COUNTY COURT
	§	
THE ESTATE OF	§	OF
	§	
ROSE HARRIS, DECEASED	§	DALLAS COUNTY, TEXAS

ORDER PROBATING WILL

On this the 24th day of September, 19__, came on to be heard the written Application of Norma Jean Harris, for the probate of the Last Will and Testament of Rose Harris, deceased, as a Muniment of Title, being an original Will dated December 5, 1970; said Application together with said Will having been filed with this Court on the 14th day of March, 19__, and said Will now being produced in Court; and it duly appearing to the Court that said Will, as alleged in said Application, is self-proved as provided in the Texas Probate Code; and the same being introduced in evidence in this cause; it is therefore ORDERED that no further proof of this execution shall be necessary or taken in this cause.

The Court finds that this Court has jurisdiction and venue of this estate, and that every notice and citation required by law has been duly issued, served and returned in the manner and for the length of time required by law, said citation being returnable this the 24th day of September, 19__; and the Court further finds that the said Rose Harris, at or before her death, was a resident citizen of Dallas

County, Texas, and had her domicile and fixed place of residence in Dallas County, Texas, and the principal estate of said Decedent was and is located in Dallas County, Texas, and that the said Rose Harris died on the 25th day of February, 19__, in Dallas, Dallas County, Texas.

The Court further finds that the Decedent, Rose Harris, was on the 5th day of December, 1970, at the time of executing such Will, over the age of eighteen (18) years; and that at such time Rose Harris was of sound mind, and that the said Rose Harris executed said instrument dated December 5, 1970, with the formalities and solemnities and under the circumstances required by law to make such Will a valid Will; and the Court finds that said Will has not been revoked by said Rose Harris and that said writing dated December 5, 1970, is and constitutes the Last Will and Testament of Rose Harris, the Decedent, and said original Will dated the 5th day of December, 1970, is entitled to probate as the Last Will and Testament of said Decedent.

And it further appearing to the Court that Norma Jean Harris was named and appointed by said Will as Independent Executrix, that said Applicant, Norma Jean Harris, is a resident of the County of Dallas, State of Texas, that four (4) years have not elapsed since the death of the said Rose Harris, that said Will hereby admitted to probate provided that no other action shall be had in the County Court in relation to said estate than the appraisement and list of claims of said estate, and in accordance with the Application on file there is no necessity for administration in said estate;

IT IS THEREFORE ORDERED, ADJUDGED AND DECREED that said written Will of Rose Harris dated the 5th day of December, 1970, on file herein, be and the same is hereby admitted to probate and record as a Muniment of Title and said Will together with the Application for probate thereof and all testimony given in this proceeding shall be recorded in the minutes of this Court.

IT IS FURTHER ORDERED, ADJUDGED AND DECREED that this Order shall constitute sufficient legal authority to all persons owing any money, having custody of any property, or acting as a registrar or transfer agent of any interest, indebtedness, property or right belonging to the estate of Rose Harris, deceased, and to persons purchasing from or otherwise dealing with the estate of Rose Harris, deceased, for payment or transfer to the persons described in said Will as entitled to receive the particular asset without administration.

DATED and ENTERED this the __________ day of ________________, 19____.

____
County Judge
Dallas County, Texas

UNIT 10

Business Law

Section A
Entities Other Than Corporations

The expression *business law* is an all-inclusive term that commonly refers to all legal practices, documents, and instruments related to the conduct of income-producing, commercial enterprises. Business entities are divided roughly into two groups: one category includes sole proprietorships and partnerships and pertains to the concept of individuals engaged in business enterprises; the other category includes corporations, which take on a life of their own and are not dependent on the survival of any participating person.

VOCABULARY

general partner (jĕn′-ər-əl pärt′-nər)	A person who conducts the business of a partnership and has unlimited liability.
limited partner (lĭm′-ə-tĭd pärt′-nər)	A person who invests capital and shares in the profits of the partnership but whose liability and share of profits are limited by the amount invested.
partnership (pärt′-nər-shĭp)	Two or more persons owning a business for common benefit and sharing in profits and losses.
power of attorney (pou′-ər ŭv ə-tûr′-nē)	An instrument by which one person gives another person the right to act in his place and stead.
proprietor (prə-prī′-ə-tər)	A person who is the sole owner of a business.

VOCABULARY-DICTATION

When two or more persons own an unincorporated business for their common benefit and share in both profits and losses, the business entity is called a <u>partnership</u>. A <u>general partner</u> is an individual who conducts the business of the partnership and has unlimited liability. A limited partner invests capital and shares in the profits of the partnership, but his liability and share of profits are limited by the amount he invested.

A proprietor is a person who is a sole owner. A business totally owned by one person is referred to as a sole proprietorship. In both a proprietorship and a partnership, if any participant dies, the business entity usually terminates at the moment of death.

If Mr. A wishes to give Mr. B the right to act on Mr. A's behalf, a power of attorney is prepared giving Mr. B this right. A power of attorney can be "limited" so as to cover one or more specific purposes; for example, to purchase a certain piece of real estate; or, it can be "general," enabling Mr. B to act for Mr. A in all matters.

SELF-TEST—UNIT 10A

1. A(n) ________________________ is an individual who conducts the business of a partnership and has unlimited liability.
2. When two or more persons own an unincorporated business for their common benefit and share in both profits and losses, the business entity is called a(n) ________________________.
3. The sole owner of a business is referred to as the ________________________.
4. An instrument giving one person the right to act on another's behalf is called a(n) ________________________.
5. A(n) ________________________ invests capital and shares in the profits of partnership, but his liability and share of profits are limited by the amount he invested.

UNIT 10A—EXERCISE 1

Partnership Agreement

PARTNERSHIP AGREEMENT

THE STATE OF TEXAS §
§
COUNTY OF DALLAS §

This Agreement of general partnership entered into on April 1, 19__, by and among Adam Wright, Eve Appleton, and A. S. Peterson (hereinafter collectively referred to as "Partners," and individually as "Partner").

1. NAME AND PURPOSE.

The Partnership shall be carried on under the name of WAP Properties. The Partnership has been formed for the purpose of owning, developing, operating, leasing and otherwise dealing with real and personal property of any kind or description. The Partnership may engage in any and all other activities as may be necessary, incidental, or convenient to carry out the business of the Partnership as contemplated by this agreement.

2. PLACE OF BUSINESS.

The principal office of the Partnership shall be located at 5404 Garden Street, Dallas, Texas, or at such other place as it shall be agreed upon by a majority in interest of the Partners from time to time.

3. PARTNERS.

The name and address of each of the Partners are as follows:

NAME	**ADDRESS**
Adam Wright	Richardson, Texas
Eve Appleton	Mesquite, Texas
A. S. Peterson	Dallas, Texas

4. TERM.

The Partnership shall commence on April 1, 19__, and shall continue until terminated as provided in this agreement.

5. CONTRIBUTIONS.

Each of the Partners has or will contribute to the initial capital of the Partnership, in cash, the amount of Twenty Thousand and No/100 Dollars ($20,000.00). An individual capital account shall be established and maintained for each Partner who shall receive an interest in the Partnership and shall be credited with the amounts of his capital contributions to the Partnership from time to time. A Partner shall not be entitled to interest on his capital contribution, or to withdraw any part of his capital account, or to receive any distribution from the Partnership, except as specifically provided herein.

6. NET PROFITS, NET LOSSES AND CASH FLOW.

(a) Profits and Losses. Subject to such adjustments as may be required pursuant to Paragraph 7 below, the net profits and net losses shall be shared by the Partners equally. The terms "net profits" and "net losses" shall mean the net profits and losses of the Partnership as determined for Federal income tax purposes by the accountant servicing the Partnership account.

(b) Cash Flow. The "cash flow of the Partnership" shall be the net profits and losses of the Partnership as defined in Paragraph 6(a) above, plus (i) depreciation and other non-cash charges deducted in determining such net profits and losses, (ii) the net proceeds from any refinancing from the Partnership's mortgages, and (iii) the net proceeds from the sale of any of the Partnership's assets, minus (i) principal payments on all mortgages, (ii) any other cash expenditures which have not been deducted in determining the net profits and losses of the Partnership, and (iii) any amount reasonably required to maintain sufficient working capital and a reasonable reserve for replacements. The cash flow of the Partnership shall be determined separately for each fiscal year and not cumulatively and, as so determined, shall be distributed in the same proportions as profits and losses are shared in accordance with Paragraph 6(a), subject to such adjustments as may be required for Paragraph 7. The cash flow shall be distributed at the discretion of the Managing Partner, but at least annually.

7. ADDITIONAL FUNDS AND ADJUSTMENTS.

(a) Call for Funds. The Partners recognize that the income produced by the Partnership's properties may be insufficient to pay the operating costs of the properties. If in the judgment of the Managing Partner, additional funds are required to pay such operating costs, the additional funds shall be called for by the Managing Partner and shall be contributed by the Partners in proportion to their capital interest in the Partnership. As used above, the term "operating costs" shall include, without limitation: principal and interest payments on Partnership loans, whether or not secured by mortgages on Partnership properties; costs of repair, maintenance and improvements; insurance premiums; and real estate taxes, assessments, and other governmental charges.

(b) Contributions for Non-defaulting Partners. If any Partner is unable or unwilling to make any or all of his proportionate contribution, then the remaining Partners who are able and willing to do so may make a contribution in excess of their proportionate share in such amounts as they may agree among themselves. If they are unable to agree, each Partner who is able and willing to make a contribution shall have the primary right to contribute that portion of such excess which the proportion of such Partner's capital interest in the Partnership bears to the aggregate capital interest of all such Partners, and the secondary right to contribute any remaining portion of such excess which is not desired to be contributed by any other Partner in the exercise of his primary right. If there is more than one (1) Partner desiring to exercise his secondary rights, he shall be entitled to contribute the remaining portion of such excess in the same proportion as stated above with regard to his primary rights.

(c) Contributions by Non-defaulting Partners. Any Partner who makes a contribution to the Partnership pursuant to Paragraph 7(b) above shall have the option to (i) treat the contributions as additional capital of the Partnership, or (ii) treat the contribution as a loan to the defaulting Partner, which election shall be made, in writing, at the time the contribution is made.

8. MANAGING PARTNER.

(a) The day-to-day affairs of the Partnership shall be handled by the Managing Partner, Adam Wright. If at any time Adam Wright is unable or unwilling to serve as Managing Partner, the successor Managing Partner of the Partnership, as well as the successor to fill any vacancy thereafter occurring in such office, shall be the first in the order named who is able and willing to serve of the following:

Eve Appleton;

A. S. Peterson.

(b) The Managing Partner shall provide such services to the operation of the Partnership business as he shall deem proper and necessary, including keeping all Partners informed of all letters, accounts, writings, and other information which shall come to his attention concerning the business of the Partnership.

(c) The Managing Partner shall keep or cause to be kept full records of each transaction of the Partnership and shall maintain such records at the principal office of the Partnership or at the principal office of the Partnership's accounting firm. Said records shall be open for inspection and examination by all Partners, or their duly authorized representative, at all reasonable times. The Managing Partner shall furnish, or cause to be furnished, to each Partner statements of financial condition of the Partnership within sixty (60) days after the end of each fiscal year of the Partnership. The fiscal year of the Partnership shall end on December 31.

(d) The Managing Partner shall not be liable to the Partnership or to any Partner for any mistake or error in judgment or for any act or omission believed in good faith to be within the scope of authority conferred by this Agreement. The Managing Partner shall be liable only for acts and/or omissions involving intentional wrongdoing.

9. VOTING.

Each Partner shall vote in proportion to his capital interest in the Partnership from time to time. Each Partner may exercise his vote by written or oral notification to the Managing Partner, in each of those instances hereinafter stated.

10. CONSENT TO OPERATIONS.

The procedure for the operation of the Partnership shall be as follows:

(a) The day-to-day affairs of the Partnership shall be handled by the Managing Partner, as hereinabove stated.

(b) The following actions shall require the vote and unanimous approval of all the Partners: (i) The purchasing and developing of new properties; (ii) The amendment of this Partnership Agreement; and (iii) The admission of new partners to the Partnership.

11. AMENDMENTS.

Amendments to this Agreement shall become effective only if in writing, signed by all the Partners.

12. TERMINATION OF PARTNERSHIP.

The Partnership shall be terminated and dissolved upon the vote of a majority in interest of the Partners. Upon the termination of the Partnership as herein provided, a full and general accounting shall be taken of the Partnership business and the affairs of the Partnership shall be wound up. Any profits or losses incurred since the previous accounting shall be divided among the Partners and shall be added to the distribution to be made to the Partners. The Managing Partner shall wind up and liquidate the Partnership by selling the Partnership assets and, after the payment of the Partnership liabilities, expenses and fees incurred in connection with such liquidation, distributing the net proceeds therefrom, in cash to the Partners in proportion to their capital interests in the Partnership.

Except as otherwise expressly provided in this Partnership Agreement, dissolution of the Partnership shall be subject to the provisions of the Texas Uniform Partnership Act, as now constituted or hereafter amended or substituted. Unless otherwise required by law or by court order and subject to the provisions of Section 14 of this Partnership Agreement, the Partnership business shall not terminate upon the occurrence of any event causing dissolution of the Partnership.

13. NOTICES.

All notices, consents and other instruments hereunder shall be in writing and mailed by certified mail, return receipt requested, postage prepaid, and shall be directed to the parties hereto at the addresses hereinabove set forth or at the last address of the parties furnished by them in writing to the Managing Partner. Notices to the personal representative of a deceased Partner's estate shall be mailed in the same manner to the last known address of such representative.

14. BINDING EFFECT.

This Agreement shall inure to the benefit of and be binding upon the parties hereto and their respective next-of-kin, legatees, administrators, executors, legal representatives, successors and permitted assigns.

IN WITNESS WHEREOF, the parties hereto have executed triplicate originals of this Agreement on this _______ day of ____________________, 19__.

____
ADAM WRIGHT

____
EVE APPLETON

____
A. S. PETERSON

Section 10B
Corporations

In the world of business and business law, a corporation is an entity, an artificial being that is able to act and contract, sue and be sued. Unlike a partnership, which disappears if one partner withdraws or dies, a corporation is an artificial being that continues to exist—with or without the original incorporators—until legally terminated.

VOCABULARY

alien corporation (ā′-lē-ən kôr-pə-rā′-shən)	A corporation that received its charter from a foreign country.
articles of incorporation (är′-tĭ-kəls ŭv ĭn-kôr′-pə-rā-shən)	The instrument setting forth the general purposes and organization of a corporation.
asset (ăs′-ĕt)	Anything of value, tangible and intangible, owned by a person or a business; for example, cash, equipment, vehicles, furniture, and goodwill.
bylaws (bī′-lôz)	The specific rules or regulations by which a corporation is managed.
charter (chär′-tər)	The authority to exist granted by the state to a corporation.
corporation (kôr-pə-rā′-shən)	A legal entity created under statutory provisions.
dissolution (dĭs-ə-lo͞o′-shən)	The termination of the existence of a legal entity, such as a partnership or a corporation.
dividends (dĭv′-ə-dĕnds)	A portion of corporate profits divided among the shareholders, in cash and/or stock.
domestic corporation (də-mĕs′-tĭk kôr-pə-rā′-shən)	A corporation doing business in the state that granted its charter.

eleemosynary corporation (ĕl′-ə-mŏs-ə-nĕr-ē kôr-pə-rā′-shən)
A corporation organized for charitable or benevolent purposes.

foreign corporation (fôr′-ĭn kôr-pə-rā′-shən)
A corporation doing business in states other than the one that granted its charter.

franchise (frăn′-chīz)
A special privilege granted by the government; a corporation is a franchise.

legal entity (lē′-gəl ĕn′-tə-tē)
A being, actual or artificial, granted the right to operate in a state.

liability (lī′-ə-bĭl-ə-tē)
Any debt or obligation of a business or individual.

liquidation (lĭk-wə-dā′-shən)
The sale and/or distribution of the assets of a business to settle its accounts with creditors and/or stockholders.

merger (mûr′-jər)
A combination of two or more corporations whereby one remains a legal entity and the other is absorbed.

net worth (nĕt wûrth)
The worth of a business or individual after deducting the liabilities from the assets.

proxy (prŏk′-sē)
The authorization for another to act for a shareholder at a meeting; also, the paper granting the authority.

quorum (kwôr′-əm)
The number of members who must be present at a meeting for business to be transacted; a majority.

retained earnings (rē′-tānd ûrn′-ĭngs)
The portion of corporate profits kept by the corporation for operating expenses or capital expenditures.

subsidiary (səb-sĭd′-ē-ăr-ē)
A company owned (by a majority of shares or interest) and controlled by another company.

VOCABULARY-DICTATION

A corporation is a legal entity created under statutory provisions. A *close or closely held corporation* is one with 35 or fewer shareholders. A *public* corporation is one for which shares of stock are sold to the general public. A subsidiary is a separate legal entity owned and controlled by another company. A corporation doing business in the state that granted its charter is referred to as a domestic corporation. Oddly enough, a foreign corporation is not a corporation from a foreign country, but rather is a corporation doing business in states other than the one granting its charter. An alien corporation is not a company from outer space; it's a corporation that received its charter from a foreign country. A corporation organized for charitable or benevolent purposes is called an eleemosynary corporation.

The first step for incorporation is to file articles of incorporation, the instrument setting forth the general purposes and organization of a corporation, with the secretary of state. After receiving and approving the articles of incorporation, the secretary of state will issue a charter, which is the authority to exist granted to a corporation by the state. A special privilege granted by the government is called a franchise. Since a corporation's existence is authorized by the state, it is a franchise; corporations pay an annual franchise tax. A being, actual or artificial, granted the right to operate in the state becomes a legal entity, with legal duties and responsibilities in and of itself.

A merger is the combining of two or more corporations whereby one continues as the legal entity and the other is absorbed and no longer exists. The specific rules or regulations by which a corporation is managed are called the corporate bylaws. Proxy has a dual meaning: it is both the authorization for another to act for a shareholder at a meeting and the paper granting this authority. The number of members, usually a simple majority, that must be present at a meeting for business to be transacted is called a quorum.

Anything of value, tangible or intangible, owned by a business (e.g., cash, equipment, vehicles, furniture, and goodwill) is considered an asset. A liability is any debt or obligation of the business. The net worth of the business is the balance after deducting liabilities from assets. If the net worth is a positive figure, dividends, a portion of corporate profits divided among shareholders, can be paid. Retained earnings is the asset account indicating the portion of corporate profits kept by the corporation for operating expenses or capital expenditures.

If things do not go well with any business other than a sole proprietorship, it is not sufficient to lock the door and go fishing. If a legal document is required to create a business entity, a formal dissolution is necessary to terminate the existence of the legal entity, be it either a partnership or a corporation. If things do not go well at all, a liquidation, or the sale and/or distribution of the assets of a business, may be necessary to settle its accounts with creditors and/or stockholders.

SELF-TEST—UNIT 10B

1. ______________________ are a portion of corporate profits divided among shareholders.
2. A(n) ______________________ is a separate legal entity owned and controlled by another company.
3. ______________________ is the portion of corporate profits kept by the corporation for operating expenses or capital expenditures.
4. The authority to exist granted to a corporation by the state is called a(n) ______________________.
5. A(n) ______________________ is any debt or obligation of the business.

6. A corporation doing business in the state that granted its charter is referred to as a(n) ________________________.
7. A(n) ________________________ is a legal entity created under statutory provisions.
8. A special privilege granted by the government is called a(n) ____________ ____________.
9. A(n) ________________________ is a corporation that received its charter from a foreign country.
10. An actual or artificial being granted the right to operate in the state becomes a(n) ________________________.
11. ________________________ is the sale and/or distribution of the assets of a business necessary to settle its accounts with creditors and/or shareholders.
12. A(n) ________________________ is the combining of two or more corporations whereby one continues as the legal entity and the other is absorbed and no longer exists.
13. A corporation organized for charitable or benevolent purposes is called a(n) ________________________.
14. A(n) ________________________ is a corporation doing business in states other than the one that granted its charter.
15. A(n) ________________________ is either the authorization for another to act for a shareholder at a meeting or the paper granting this authority.
16. Anything of value, tangible or intangible, owned by a business (i.e., cash, equipment, vehicles, furniture, and goodwill) is considered a(n) _______ ________________.
17. The specific rules or regulations by which a corporation is managed are called the corporate ________________________.

18. The ______________________ is the instrument setting forth the general purposes and organization of the corporation.
19. The ______________________ of the business is the balance after deducting the liabilities from the assets.
20. ______________________ is the termination of the existence of a legal entity, either a partnership or a corporation.
21. The number of members, usually a simple majority, that must be present at a meeting for business to be transacted is called a(n) ______________________.

UNIT 10B—EXERCISE 1

Articles of Incorporation

ARTICLES OF INCORPORATION
OF
MOORE FINANCIAL CORPORATION

The undersigned, a natural person of the age of eighteen (18) years or more, who is a citizen of the State of Texas, acting as incorporator of a corporation under the Texas Business Corporation Act, hereby adopts the following Articles of Incorporation for such corporation:

ARTICLE ONE

The name of the corporation is MOORE FINANCIAL CORPORATION.

ARTICLE TWO

The period of its duration is perpetual.

ARTICLE THREE

The purpose or purposes for which the corporation is organized are:

To engage in and transact any or all lawful business; provided, however, that nothing stated above authorizes the corporation to be organized for or to transact business in this state which is prohibited by Article 2.01B of the Texas Business Corporation Act, as now written or as hereafter amended.

To buy, sell and deal in personal property, real property and services.

ARTICLE FOUR

The aggregate number of shares which the corporation has the authority to issue is 100,000 shares of the par value of $10.00 each. The shares are designated Common Stock and have identical rights and privileges in every respect.

ARTICLE FIVE

The corporation will not commence business until it has received for the issuance of its shares consideration of a value of One Thousand Dollars ($1,000.00), consisting of money, labor done, or property actually received.

ARTICLE SIX

Directors shall be elected by majority vote. Cumulative voting shall not be permitted.

ARTICLE SEVEN

The post office address of the initial registered office of the corporation is 9304 Woodsy Road, Suite 161, Dallas, Texas 75243, and the name of its registered agent at such address is John Q. Moore.

ARTICLE EIGHT

The number of directors constituting the initial Board of Directors is three (3); however, thereafter the Bylaws shall fix the number at not less than one (1) and not more than seven (7). The name and address of the persons who are to serve as directors until the first annual meeting of the shareholders, or until their successors are elected and qualified, are:

NAME	**ADDRESS**
John Q. Moore	2412 Cochise Drive Mesquite, TX 75150
Rene I. Tanner	605 Goodland Richardson, TX 75081
Sally Sue Moore	2412 Cochise Drive Mesquite, TX 75150

The name and address of the incorporator is:

NAME	**ADDRESS**
John Q. Moore	2412 Cochise Drive Mesquite, TX 75150

ARTICLE NINE

No holder of any stock of the corporation shall be entitled as a matter of right to purchase or subscribe for any part of any stock of the corporation authorized by these Articles or of any additional stock of any class to be issued by reason of any increase of the authorized stock of the corporation, or of any bonds, certificates of indebtedness, debentures, warrants, options, or other securities convertible into any class of stock of the corporation. Any stock authorized by these Articles or any such additional authorized issue of any stock or securities convertible into any stock may be issued and disposed of by the Board of Directors to such persons, firms, corporations, or associations for such consideration upon such terms and in such manner as the Board of Directors may in its discretion determine without offering any thereof on the same terms or on any terms to the shareholders then of record or to any class of shareholders, provided only that issuance may not be inconsistent with any provision of law or with any of the provisions of these Articles.

ARTICLE TEN

The initial Bylaws shall be adopted by the Board of Directors. The power to alter, amend, or repeal the Bylaws or adopt new Bylaws, subject to repeal or change by action of the shareholders, shall be vested in the Board of Directors.

ARTICLE ELEVEN

The corporation shall indemnify any person who is or was a director, officer, agent, or employee of the corporation, and any person who serves or served at the corporation's request as a director, officer, agent, employee, partner, or trustee of another corporation, partnership, joint venture, trust, or other enterprise.

IN WITNESS WHEREOF, I have hereunto set my hand, this ________ day of ______________________, 19__.

____

John Q. Moore

SWORN TO on the ________ day of ______________________, 19__ by the above named incorporator.

____

Notary Public in the State of Texas

My Commission Expires: _______________________________

Printed Name of Notary

____

UNIT 10B—EXERCISE 2

Letter Filing Articles of Incorporation

MOORE FINANCIAL CORPORATION
9304 Woodsy Road Suite 161
Dallas, Texas 75243

Date

Corporate Division
Office of Secretary of State
State of Texas
P. O. Box 13697
Austin, Texas 78711

Re: Moore Financial Corporation

Gentlemen:

Enclosed please find original and one (1) copy of Articles of Incorporation for the above referenced corporation, together with cashier's check in the amount of $310 for the filing fee of $200, prepayment on franchise tax of $100, and special handling fee of $10.

Your attention in this matter is appreciated.

Very truly yours,

John Q. Moore

JQM:

Enclosures

UNIT 10B—EXERCISE 3

Unanimous Consent in Lieu of Organizational Meeting

UNANIMOUS CONSENT IN LIEU OF
ORGANIZATIONAL MEETING
OF
MOORE FINANCIAL CORPORATION

We, the undersigned, being all of the directors named in the Articles of Incorporation of MOORE FINANCIAL CORPORATION, a Texas corporation (the "Corporation"), pursuant to the provisions of Section 9.10 of the Texas Business Corporation Act, do, by our unanimous consent, take the following corporate action and adopt the following resolutions, which corporate action and resolutions shall have the same force and effect as a unanimous vote of all of the directors of the Corporation at a formal organizational meeting of the Board of Directors of said Corporation:

RESOLVED, that the Articles of Incorporation, having been approved and filed in the office of the Secretary of State of Texas on June ___________, 19___ be placed in the Minute Book of this Corporation.

* * * * *

RESOLVED, that John Q. Moore, Rene I. Tanner, and Sally Sue Moore having been designated as directors of the Corporation by the Articles of Incorporation until the first annual meeting of shareholders or until their successors are elected and qualified, do accept the office of Director of the Corporation, such acceptance being evidenced by their respective signatures below.

* * * * *

RESOLVED, that the Bylaws submitted to each director of this Corporation be, and the same hereby are, adopted for and as the Bylaws of this Corporation, and the Secretary of this Corporation be, and the same hereby is, directed to cause a copy of the Bylaws to be inserted in the Minute Book of this Corporation.

* * * * *

RESOLVED, that the form of certificate representing the shares of the Common Stock of this Corporation, which certificate has been submitted to this meeting, be, and it hereby is, approved and adopted as the form of certificate to represent the shares of Common Stock of the Corporation.

* * * * *

RESOLVED, that the seal, an impression of which is affixed hereto, be, and it hereby is, adopted as the official seal of the Corporation.

(*Instruction:* Leave space in your document to imprint the Corporate Seal)

* * * * *

RESOLVED, that the following individuals be, and they hereby are, elected to the offices set forth opposite their respective names, to serve as such until the first meeting of the Board of Directors of the Corporation following the next annual meeting of shareholders or until their respective successors are elected and qualify:

NAME	**OFFICE(S)**
John Q. Moore	President
Sally Sue Moore	Vice President/Secretary

* * * * *

RESOLVED, that the offer of John Q. Moore to pay $10,000 as the total purchase price of 1,000 shares of the Common Stock, $10.00 par value, of the Corporation be, and it hereby is, accepted; and

FURTHER RESOLVED, that upon payment in cash to this Corporation of an aggregate of $10,000, the President and Secretary of this Corporation are hereby authorized to issue to John Q. Moore 1,000 shares of the $10.00 par value Common Stock of this Corporation.

* * * * *

RESOLVED, that regular bank accounts in the name of the Corporation be opened from time to time as necessary or appropriate, wherein may be deposited any of the funds of this Corporation and from which withdrawals are hereby authorized in the name of this Corporation by the signatures of such individual or individuals as the President shall designate; and

FURTHER RESOLVED, that the Secretary of this Corporation be, and the same hereby is, authorized to certify to such bank accounts in such form as said banks may customarily require, and such resolutions shall be inserted in the Minute Book of the Corporation following these minutes as if set forth herein in full; and

FURTHER RESOLVED, that the President of this Corporation be, and the same hereby is, authorized to borrow in the name and on behalf of the Corporation such funds in such amounts from such persons or such lending institutions as he, in his discretion, deems in the best interests of this Corporation; and

FURTHER RESOLVED, that the Secretary and any Assistant Secretary be, and each hereby is, authorized to certify to such lender as it may customarily require and such resolutions so certified shall be deemed to be copied in these minutes as fully as if set forth herein in full.

* * * * *

RESOLVED, that the fiscal year for this Corporation shall commence on the 1st day of May each year and shall end on the 30th day of April of each year.

* * * * *

RESOLVED, that the election to impose the tax directly on the income of the owners of the stock by the means of Sub-Chapter S of the Internal Revenue Code is adopted and the Corporation so consented to this election. The officers are authorized and directed to do all things necessary and appropriate to carry out the adoption of Sub-Chapter S for the Corporation and to file the appropriate Form 2553.

* * * * *

RESOLVED, that the Treasurer of this Corporation, be and the same hereby is, authorized to pay out of the funds of this Corporation all of the fees and expenses incurred necessary to the organization of this Corporation.

* * * * *

DATED this ______ day of ____________________, 19__.

____
John Q. Moore

____
Address

____
Rene I. Tanner

____
Address

____
Sally Sue Moore

____
Address

UNIT 10B—EXERCISE 4

Bylaws

BYLAWS
OF
MOORE FINANCIAL CORPORATION

ARTICLE I

— OFFICES —

Section 1.1 The registered office of the Corporation shall be at 9304 Woodsy Road, Suite 161, Dallas, County of Dallas, State of Texas, and the name of the registered agent of the Corporation at such address is John Q. Moore.

Section 1.2 The Corporation may also have offices at such other places both within and without the State of Texas as the Board of Directors may from time to time determine or the business of the Corporation may require.

ARTICLE II

— MEETING OF SHAREHOLDERS —

Section 2.1 Meetings of shareholders for any purpose may be held at such time and place, within or without the State of Texas, as shall be stated in the notice of the meeting or in a duly executed waiver of notice thereof.

Section 2.2 An annual meeting of the shareholders shall be held each year on the first Wednesday of the fourth month following the end of the Corporation's prior fiscal year. The first annual meeting of shareholders shall be held in the calendar year immediately succeeding the year in which the Corporation was incorporated. If such annual meeting date falls upon a legal holiday, then the annual meeting shall be held upon the next secular day following such holiday. At each annual meeting, the shareholders shall elect a Board of Directors and shall transact such other business as may be properly brought before the meeting.

Section 2.3 Special meetings of the shareholders, for any purpose or purposes, unless otherwise prescribed by statute or by the Articles of Incorporation, or by these Bylaws, may be called by the president, Board of Directors, or the holders of not less than ten percent (10%) of all the shares entitled to vote at the meetings. Business transacted at all special meetings shall be confined to the objects stated in the notice of the meeting.

Section 2.4 The holders of a majority of the shares issued and outstanding and entitled to vote thereat, present in person or represented by proxy, shall be requisite and shall constitute a quorum at all meetings of the shareholders for the transaction of business except as otherwise provided by statute, by the Articles of Incorporation or by these Bylaws.

ARTICLE III

– DIRECTORS –

Section 3.1 The business and affairs of the Corporation shall be managed by its Board of Directors who may exercise all such powers of the Corporation and do all such lawful acts and things as are not by statute or by the Articles of Incorporation or by these Bylaws directed or required to be done by the shareholders.

Section 3.2 The initial Board of Directors shall consist of the number of directors specified in the Articles of Incorporation. None of the directors need be a shareholder or resident of the State of Texas. At each annual meeting of the shareholders, the shareholders may change the number of directors who shall serve for the ensuing year and thereafter until the number shall again be changed by vote of the shareholders.

— MEETINGS OF THE BOARD OF DIRECTORS —

Section 3.3 The first meeting of each newly elected Board shall be held without further notice immediately following the annual meeting of the shareholders.

Section 3.4 Regular meetings of the Board of Directors may be held without notice at such time and place as shall be determined by the board.

Section 3.5 Special meetings of the Board of Directors may be called by the president on three days' notice to each director, either personally or by mail or by telegram.

Section 3.6 At all meetings of the Board of Directors, the presence of a majority of the directors shall be necessary and sufficient to constitute a quorum for the transaction of business, and the act of a majority of the directors present at any meeting at which there is a quorum shall be the act of the Board of Directors, except as may be otherwise specifically provided by statute or by the Articles of Incorporation or by these By-laws. If a quorum shall not be present at any meeting, the directors present thereat may adjourn the meeting from time to time without notice other than announcement at the meeting until a quorum shall be present.

— COMPENSATION OF DIRECTORS —

Section 3.7 Directors, as such, shall not receive any stated salary for their services but, by resolution of the Board, a fixed sum and expenses of attendance, if any, may be allowed for attendance at each regular or special meeting of the Board, provided that nothing herein contained shall be construed to preclude any director from serving the Corporation in any other capacity and receiving compensation therefor.

(*Note:* Additional typical articles of Corporate Bylaws would be as follows:)

ARTICLE IV

— NOTICES —

ARTICLE V

— OFFICERS —

ARTICLE VI

— CERTIFICATES REPRESENTING SHARES —

— REGISTERED SHAREHOLDERS —

ARTICLE VII

— DIVIDENDS —

ARTICLE VIII

— GENERAL PROVISIONS —

ARTICLE IX

— AMENDMENTS —

Section 9.1 These Bylaws may be altered, amended, or repealed at any meeting of the Board of Directors at which a quorum is present, by the affirmative vote of a majority of the directors, provided notice of the proposed alteration, amendment, or repeal be contained in the notice of such meeting (or such notice shall have been waived).

The above and foregoing Bylaws contained on ____________ (_____) pages are hereby authenticated as the Bylaws adopted at the organizational meeting held by unanimous consent under date of ____, 19__.

____
Secretary

Section 10C
Contracts

The term *contract* encompasses the promise to do or not to do some legal act for sufficient consideration. A contract may be written or oral; however, a written contract ensures understanding between the parties of the entire agreement and is more easily enforced. Under contract law, there are certain elements statutorily required for a valid contract; if any one element is not included, the contract is voidable.

VOCABULARY

acceptance (ak-sĕp′-təns)	Agreement to the offer received by one person from another; an essential element of a contract.
breach of contract (brēch ŭv kŏn′-trăkt)	Failure to perform all or part of an agreement.
caveat emptor (kā′-vē-ăt ĕmp′-tôr)	Latin, meaning "let the buyer beware"; a legal maxim that implies the buyer is responsible and buys at his own risk.
collateral (kə-lăt′-ər-əl)	Something pledged by the borrower to ensure repayment of a loan.
competent parties (kŏm′-pə-tənt pär′-tēz)	Persons entering into a contract must be legally competent to do so; an essential element for a valid contract.
consideration (kən-sĭd-ə-rā′-shən)	The benefit or incentive for entering into a contract; an essential element for a valid contract.
contract (kŏn′-trăkt)	An agreement between two or more persons (including corporations and partnerships) who promise to do or not to do specific things.
covenant (kŭv′-ə-nənt)	(n) An agreement; (v) to agree.

escalator clause (ĕs′kə-lā-tər klôz)	A clause within a contract that states that if costs increase or decrease, payments may increase or decrease accordingly.
execute (ĕk′sĭ-kyo͞ot)	To put into effect or carry out the terms of a contract.
indemnify (ĭn-dĕm′nə-fī)	To agree contractually to pay for loss or injury.
offer (ô′fər)	A proposal made by one person to another for a potential agreement; an essential element of a contract.
option (ŏp′shən)	An agreement whereby a person can buy, sell, or lease something within a specified time.
performance (pər-fôr′məns)	The fulfillment of the terms of a contract.
quid pro quo (kwĭd prō kwō)	Latin, meaning "something for something"; refers to the consideration in a contract.
rescind (rĭ-sĭnd′)	To cancel or void a contract.
subrogation (sŭb-rə-gā′shən)	The assignment of the rights of one party to a contract to another who was not a party to the contract.
surety (sho͝or′ə-tē)	A person who agrees to be responsible for a debt in the event the borrower defaults on payment.
vitiate (vĭsh′ē-āt)	To destroy the legality of a contract.

VOCABULARY-DICTATION

The word covenant can be used either as a noun, meaning "an agreement," or as a verb, meaning "to agree." An agreement between two or more persons (including corporations and partnerships) who promise to do or not to do specific things is called a contract. For a contract to be binding, there are several elements that are essential. These include:

1. The persons entering into a contract must be legally competent to do so; hence, they must be competent parties;
2. An offer or a proposal must be made by one person to another for a potential agreement;
3. There must be acceptance, or agreement, to the offer received by one person from another; and
4. There must be consideration, which is the benefit or incentive for entering into a contract.

The Latin phrase quid pro quo, meaning "something for something," refers to the consideration in a contract. An option is an agreement whereby a person can buy, sell, or lease something within a specified time.

When contractual parties carry out the terms of the agreement, they are said to execute the contract. Subrogation is the assignment of the rights of one party to a contract to another who was not a party to the contract.

Fulfillment of the terms of a contract is called performance. Failure to perform all or part of an agreement is labeled breach of contract. The Latin phrase caveat emptor, which means "let the buyer beware," is a legal maxim that implies the buyer is responsible and buys at his own risk.

Collateral is something pledged by the borrower to ensure repayment of a loan. A clause within a contract that states that if costs increase or decrease, payments may increase or decrease accordingly is called an escalator clause. If one enters into a contract agreeing to indemnify someone else, he is agreeing to pay for any loss or injury. A surety is a person who agrees to be responsible for a debt in the event the borrower defaults on payment.

If a person rescinds a contract, he cancels or voids the contract. On the other hand, if a contract is vitiated, the legality of the contract is destroyed.

SELF-TEST—UNIT 10C

1. Fulfillment of the terms of a contract is called ________________________.
2. An agreement between two or more persons (including corporations and partnerships) who promise to do or not to do specific things is called a(n) ________________________.
3. A(n) ________________________ is a person who agrees to be responsible for a debt in the event the borrower defaults on payment.
4. A(n) ________________________ is an agreement whereby a person can buy, sell, or lease something within a specified time.
5. The Latin phrase ________________________ means "let the buyer beware" and is a legal maxim that implies the buyer is responsible and buys at his own risk.
6. The persons entering into a contract must be legally ____________ ____________.
7. To ________________________ a contract is to destroy the legality of the contract.
8. ________________________ is the benefit or incentive for entering into a contract.

9. To ______________________ a contract is to cancel or void the contract.
10. ______________________ is something pledged by the borrower to ensure repayment of a loan.
11. ______________________ means "something for something" and refers to the consideration in a contract.
12. Failure to perform all or part of an agreement is labeled ______________________.
13. When an agreement is ______________________, the parties agree to put into effect or carry out the terms of the contract.
14. A(n) ______________________ is a proposal made by one person to another for a potential agreement.
15. ______________________ is the assignment of the rights of one party to a contract to another who was not a party to the contract.
16. ______________________ is agreement to the offer received by one person from another.
17. A clause within a contract that states that if costs increase or decrease, payments may increase or decrease accordingly is called a(n) ______________________.
18. The word ______________________ can mean either "an agreement" or "to agree."
19. If one agrees by contract to ______________________ someone else, he is agreeing to pay for any loss or injury.

UNIT 10C—EXERCISE 1

Rental Agreement

Re: Rental Agreement

Blue Sky Telecommunications agrees to rent a telephone system which will include ______________________________

____

to ____. The rental each month will be $______________ plus state sales tax.

If said equipment is rented for a period of ______ (___) months, _____________________________ will have the option to buy the equipment for the price of $_______. However, if the equipment is not purchased, a new agreement will be necessary.

During the rental period ______________________________ will provide insurance coverage on said equipment which shall include fire and lightning, power surge, extended coverage, theft, and vandalism. ______________________________ will not at any time be responsible for more than the amount due for the remaining months of this rental agreement.

A one (1) year warranty on the equipment will be provided as well as a thirty (30) day warranty on labor. Repair and replacement cost will be at a rate of $50.00 plus state sales tax for the first hour and $35.00 plus state sales tax for each additional hour; replacement parts will be additional charges.

This agreement will be effective _______________, 19__.

The first month's rent will be due _______________, 19__.

_____________________________ _____________________________

Blue Sky Telecommunications, Lessor | Lessee

Ralph E. Williams, Owner

UNIT 10C—EXERCISE 2

Lien Waiver

LIEN WAIVER

OWNER: ____

PROJECT NAME: ____

LOCATION: ____

GENERAL CONTRACTOR: ROBERTSON ROOFING COMPANY
19304 Main Street Suite 101
Dallas, Texas 752483

The undersigned does hereby certify that through _________, 19__ the undersigned has performed labor and/or furnished materials for the construction of improvements on the above-described project at a price to such date of $________________, and in consideration of the payment to the undersigned of such sum, the receipt of which is hereby acknowledged, the undersigned does hereby release and waive all liens and claims to liens which the undersigned may have as a result of the performance of such labor and/or the furnishing of such materials. The undersigned further certifies that the last date on which the undersigned furnished such labor and/or materials was ________________, 19__, and that the undersigned has paid in full all laborers and suppliers furnishing work or materials to the undersigned in connection with such project.

ROBERTSON ROOFING COMPANY

By: ________________________
Robert Robertson - Owner

Dated: _________________________

ACKNOWLEDGMENT

STATE OF TEXAS §
§
COUNTY OF DALLAS §

Before me, the undersigned authority, on this day personally appeared Robert Robertson, the Owner of Robertson Roofing Company, a sole proprietorship, known to me to be the person whose name is subscribed to the foregoing instrument, and acknowledged to me that he executed the same for the purposes and consideration therein expressed.

GIVEN UNDER MY HAND AND SEAL OF OFFICE, this _______ day of ______________________, 19__.

____
Notary Public, State of Texas

My Commission Expires:

____
Printed Name of Notary

____

UNIT 10C—EXERCISE 3

Assignment of Oil, Gas and Mineral Lease

ASSIGNMENT OF OIL, GAS AND MINERAL LEASE

THE STATE OF TEXAS	§	
	§	KNOW ALL MEN BY THESE PRESENTS:
COUNTY OF DALLAS	§	

THAT, MOORE FINANCIAL CORPORATION, of Dallas, Texas, for and in consideration of Ten Dollars ($10.00) and other good and valuable consideration, the receipt and sufficiency of which is hereby acknowledged and confessed, has BARGAINED, SOLD, TRANSFERRED and ASSIGNED, and by these presents does, BARGAIN, SELL, TRANSFER, and ASSIGN to CAPITOL OIL CO., whose address is P.O. Box 11925, Dallas, Texas 75206, with all taxes, royalties and overrides duly paid, all of its right, title and interest in and to those certain oil and gas leases described in Exhibit "A" attached hereto and made a part hereof (hereinafter collectively referred to as the Subject Leases), together with all equipment, fixtures, and personal property, if any, located in, on and about and used in connection with, and designated the BARNEY DEEPRIGHTS Lease #1 well and equipment.

The interest herein assigned in the Subject Leases is subject to and burdened by the Lessor's reserved royalty and overriding royalties which together aggregate an undivided .26562425 of production.

As a moving part of the consideration for this agreement, Assignee assumes the obligation to properly plug and abandon the existing wellbore situated on lands covered by the Subject Leases in accordance with the terms and provisions of said leases and the rules and regulations of the Texas Railroad Commission.

The plugging obligation assumed hereunder by Assignee shall be deemed covenant running with the Subject Leases and shall be binding upon the successors, legal representatives and assigns of the Assignee.

TO HAVE AND TO HOLD the undivided interest herein assigned unto the Assignee and its successors, legal representatives and assigns, forever, subject to the terms and provisions of the Subject Leases and the above referred to instruments, and the undersigned does hereby bind itself, its successors and assigns, to WARRANT and FOREVER DEFEND, all and singular, the same unto the said Assignee and its successors, legal representatives and assigns, against the legal claim or claims of all persons whomsoever claiming or to claim the same or any part thereof, by, through and under the undersigned, but not otherwise.

DATED this ________ day of ______________________, 19__, but effective as of the 1st day of ______________________, 19__, at 7:00 a.m.

MOORE FINANCIAL CORPORATION

By: ________________________
John Q. Moore, President

THE STATE OF TEXAS §
§
COUNTY OF DALLAS §

This instrument was acknowledged before me on the ______ day of ____________, 19__, by JOHN Q. MOORE, of MOORE FINANCIAL CORPORATION, on behalf of the company.

____
Notary Public, State of Texas

My Commission Expires:

____
Printed Name of Notary

____

UNIT 11

Real Estate Law

Real estate law covers all statutes, rules, and regulations relative to *real property*, defined as land and structures on the land that are permanent in nature and not easily moved, such as houses, barns, and so on. Real property has also been interpreted by statute to include properties that make up the land in its natural state. This includes minerals, oil and gas, and underground water.

VOCABULARY

abstract (ăb-străkt′)	The history of the title to real property, including past owners and any liens or encumbrances.
ad valorem (ăd və-lôr′-əm)	Latin; taxes assessed based on the value of the item being taxed.
adverse possession (ăd-vûrs′ pə-zĕsh′-ən)	The possession of another's land for a specific time after which the one in possession can claim title.
amortize (ăm′-ər-tīz)	To arrange for the payment of a debt by installments.
appurtenance (ə-pûr′tn-əns)	Something that is permanently attached to principal property.
assessment (ə-sĕs′-mənt)	The valuation of property, real or personal, for purposes of taxation.
condemnation (kŏn-dĕm-nā′-shən)	The forced sale of private property to the government for public use.
convey (kən-vā′)	To transfer title to real property from one person to another.
conveyance (kən-vā′-əns)	The document or instrument whereby property is transferred from one person to another.
deed (dēd)	The document used to convey title to real property from one person to another.

domain (dō-mān′)	The ownership of real property.
easement (ēz′-mənt)	The right to specific use of land of another; most frequently for utilities and roads, and usually for governmental purposes.
eminent domain (ĕm′-ə-nənt dō-mān′)	The right or power of government and certain public corporations to purchase private property for public use or public necessity.
encumbrance (ĕn-kŭm′-brəns)	Any indebtedness, charge, or lien against a piece of real property; for example, a mortgage.
escrow (ĕs-krō′)	A deposit of something, usually cash, with a third person, to be held until some condition is met.
eviction (ĭ-vĭk′-shən)	The legal removal of a tenant from rented or leased property.
fee simple (fē- sĭm′-pəl)	To have absolute and unconditional ownership to real property.
fixture (fĭks′-chər)	Personal property attached to land or a building.
foreclosure (fôr-klō′-zhər)	The termination of the rights of the owner/ mortgagor, by selling the mortgaged property at public sale.
grantee (grăn-tē′)	One who receives a right to or a transfer of property.
grantor (grăn′-tər)	One who gives a right to or transfers property.
homestead (hōm′-stĕd)	A family-occupied house with surrounding land protected by law from claims of creditors.
hypothecate (hī-pŏth′-ĭ-kāt)	To mortgage or pledge property.
joint tenancy (joint tĕn′-ən-sē)	A special type of property ownership wherein ownership reverts to the survivor.
lessee (lĕ-sē′)	A person who leases property from another; a tenant.
lessor (lĕs′-ôr)	An owner of property who leases it to another; a landlord.
lien (lēn)	A claim against property, usually because money was lent and the property was pledged as security; also, for unpaid taxes.
mortgage note (môr′-gĭj nōt)	A promissory note, usually related to money borrowed to buy property.
mortgagee (môr-gĭ-jē′)	A person who lends money and receives another's property as collateral, evidenced by a note and deed of trust.
mortgagor (môr-gĭ-jôr′)	A person who borrows money using his property as collateral and signs a note and deed of trust to reflect his indebtedness.
notice to quit (nō′-tĭs tōō kwĭt)	A written notice from a landlord to a tenant requiring that the property be vacated within a certain time.

plat (plăt)	A map showing how a tract of land is divided into lots or parcels.
possession (pə-zĕsh′-ən)	Ownership or control of property for one's own use.
public domain (pŭb′-lĭk dō-mān′)	Property that is owned by the government.
quitclaim deed (kwĭt′-klām dēd)	A deed that transfers a person's interest, if any exists, in real property.
real property (re′-əl prŏp′-ər-tē)	Land and any permanent structures on the land.
recording (rĭ-kôr′-dĭng)	Copying an instrument into the public records, usually done by the county recorder.
title (tīt′l)	Ownership of real property; proof of right to ownership.
warranty deed (wôr-ən-tē dēd)	A deed that guarantees that the person transferring real property has a valid, clear title to it.

VOCABULARY-DICTATION

This unit relates to real property, which is land and all permanent structures on the land. A plat is a map that shows how a tract of land is divided into lots or parcels. Any structure permanently attached to land is referred to as an appurtenance; for example, a barn or a well. A fixture is personal property attached to land or a building; for example, the lights and stalls within a barn.

Title is a simple term meaning ownership of real property and proof of the right to ownership. The history of title to real property including past owners, and any liens or encumbrances, is called an abstract of title.

In the purchase of real property, the grantee is the one who receives a right to or a transfer of the property. The grantor is the one who gives a right to or who transfers the property. Title in a purchase of real property by a husband and wife is usually vested in a joint tenancy, which is a special type of property ownership wherein ownership reverts to the survivor. A family-occupied house that includes the surrounding land and is protected by law from claims of creditors is called a homestead. In many Texas counties, there is also a property tax reduction on homesteaded property.

In the purchase of real property, the buyer often hypothecates, or mortgages or pledges, property as collateral. A mortgage note is the promissory note, usually related to money borrowed to buy property. A claim against property, usually because money was lent and the property was pledged as security, is referred to as a lien against the property. A person who lends money using another's property as collateral is the mortgagee; whereas the individual who uses his property as collateral to borrow money is the mortgagor.

Before a person can transfer property, he must have possession, which is ownership or control of property for one's own use. When title is transferred, the seller signs a warranty deed guaranteeing that as the transferor he has a valid, clear title to the real property. A deed that transfers a person's interest, if any exists, in real property is called a quitclaim deed. This type of deed transfers only one's interest in property; it does not warrant or guarantee title.

When title is conveyed, the title to the real property is transferred from one person to another. A conveyance is a document or instrument whereby property is transferred from one person to another. A deed is a document used to convey title to real property from one person to another. The terms conveyance and deed are interchangeable, although deed is more commonly used. When property is placed in escrow, a deposit of something, usually earnest money, has been made with a third person, to be held until some condition is met.

Domain is the ownership of real property. Any indebtedness, charge, or lien against a piece of real property is an encumbrance. If one has title in fee simple, he has absolute and unconditional ownership to real property. Often, in wills, property is left to a beneficiary in *fee simple,* which means the beneficiary has unconditional title to the property.

After any transfer of real property, the instruments involved should be recorded. Recording is the copying of the instrument(s) into the public records. This is usually done by the county recorder.

Ad valorem, a Latin phrase, means that taxes are assessed based on the value of the item being taxed, which may be either real or personal property. The valuation, or assessment, of property, real or personal, establishes the base value of the property for taxation purposes. If the property is amortized, the payment of the debt on the property is made by installments and capitalized for tax purposes.

The right to use the land someone else owns in a specific way—for example, electric power line—is referred to as an easement. Public domain is property that is owned by the government. This would include all the national parks. Eminent domain is the right or power of government to purchase private property for public use or public necessity. If no amicable agreement can be reached, the government will file a condemnation suit, which is a forced sale of private property to the government for public use. An individual can claim title of another's land under the law of adverse possession, by which the individual, having had possession of another's land for a specific time, has the legal right to claim title.

A lessee is a person who leases property from another. The owner, or landlord, who leases property to a lessee is the lessor. A lease is a written agreement to rent and to occupy property for a specific period of time. *Rental* usually implies occupying property for a short term on a month-to-month basis. When rented or leased property is involved, a written notice from a landlord/lessor to a tenant/lessee requiring that the leased property be vacated within a certain time is termed a notice to quit. It is necessary to give this written notice before the legal removal or eviction of a lessee/tenant from leased property can be effected.

If payments on the purchase of real property are delinquent, foreclosure is the process by which the rights of the mortgagor are terminated and the mortgagee is entitled to resell the mortgaged property.

SELF-TEST—UNIT 11

1. When title is transferred, the seller signs a(n) ______________________, which guarantees that the person transferring the real property has a valid, clear title to it.

2. The history of title to real property, including past owners and any liens or encumbrances, is called a(n) ______________________ of title.

3. A(n) ______________________ is a map showing how a tract of land is divided into lots or parcels.

4. Any indebtedness, charge, or lien against a piece of real property is a(n) ______________________.

5. An individual who lends money to someone using that person's property as collateral is called the ______________________.

6. ______________________ is a simple term that means ownership of real property and proof of the right to ownership.

7. A(n) ______________________ is the document used to convey title to real property from one person to another.

8. In the purchase of real property, the ______________________ is the one who receives a right to or a transfer of the property.

9. A(n) ______________________ is personal property attached to land or a building; for example, the lights and stalls within a barn.

10. A family-occupied house that includes the surrounding land and is protected by law from claims of creditors is called a(n) ______________________.

11. ______________________ is the ownership of real property.

12. A(n) ______________________ is the promissory note related to money borrowed to buy property.

13. The ______________________ is the one who gives a right to or who transfers the property.

14. A person must have ______________________, which is ownership or control of property for one's own use, before he can transfer the property.

15. This unit relates to ______________________, which is defined as land and permanent structures on the land.

16. A(n) ______________________ is a person who borrows money using his property as collateral.

17. A deed that transfers a person's interest, if any exists, in real property is called a(n) ______________________.

18. Something permanently attached to land is referred to as a(n) ____________ ____________; for example, a barn.

19. ______________________ is the right or power of government and certain public corporations to purchase private property for public use or public necessity.

20. A(n) ______________________ is the document or instrument whereby property is transferred from one person to another.

21. Title in a purchase of real property by a husband and wife is usually vested in a(n) ______________________, which is a special type of property ownership wherein ownership reverts to the survivor.

22. When property is placed in ______________________, a deposit of something, usually earnest money, has been made with a third person, to be held until some condition is met.

23. In the purchase of real property, the buyer often ______________________, or mortgages or pledges, property as collateral.

24. If no amicable agreement can be reached to buy a private property for public use, the government will file a(n) ______________________ suit, which is a forced sale of private property to the government for public use.

25. If one has title in ______________________, he has absolute and unconditional ownership to real property.

26. A claim against property, usually because money was lent and the property was pledged as security, is referred to as a(n) ______________________ against the property.

27. ______________________ is the copying of the instrument(s) into the public records, which is usually done by the county recorder.

28. The owner, or landlord, of property who leases it to a lessee is the ______________________.

29. The valuation, or ______________________, of property, real or personal, establishes the tax base of the property.

30. The right to specific use of land of another; most frequently, for roads and utilities; for example, an electric power line, is referred to as a(n) ______________________.

31. When title is ______________________, the title to real property is transferred from one person to another.

32. ______________________ is property that is owned by the government.

33. If property payments are in default, ______________________ is the process to terminate the rights of the mortgagor and to take and sell the mortgaged property.

34. An individual can claim title of another's land under the law of ______________________, by which the individual, having had possession of another's land for a specific time, has the legal right to claim title.

35. A(n) ______________________, or tenant, is a person who leases property from another.

36. When rented property is involved, a written notice from the landlord to the tenant to vacate the leased property within a certain time is termed a(n) ______________________.

37. A Latin phrase, ______________________, means that taxes are assessed based on the value of the item being taxed, which may be either real or personal property.

38. It is necessary to give written notice before the legal removal, or ______ ________________, of a tenant from leased property can be effected.

39. If the property is ______________________, the payment of the debt on the property is made by installments and capitalized for tax purposes.

UNIT 11—EXERCISE 1

Warranty Deed

WARRANTY DEED

STATE OF TEXAS §
§ KNOW ALL MEN BY THESE PRESENTS:
COUNTY OF DALLAS §

That SHERMAN BAILEY of the County of Dallas, State of Texas, hereinafter referred to as GRANTOR, for and in consideration of the sum of TEN AND NO/100TH DOLLARS ($10.00) cash and other good and valuable consideration, the receipt of which is hereby acknowledged, paid by JOHN S. HAWKINS, of the County of Dallas, State of Texas, hereinafter referred to as GRANTEE, has Granted, Sold, and Conveyed, and by these presents does Grant, Sell, and Convey, unto the said GRANTEE of the County of Dallas, State of Texas, and unto his successors and assigns, a single tract and parcel of land lying and situated in Dallas County, Texas, more fully described as follows:

All that part of Lot 12, Block D, of the Old Donation Addition to the City of Mesquite, Dallas County, Texas, and more fully described as follows, being the same land conveyed to William Barry by Bob Forest as recorded in Vol. 988, Pg. 541, Dallas County Deed Records:

BEGINNING at the Northwest corner of Lot 12, Block D in South line of Public Square, the same being the Northeast corner of Lot 11, Block D;

THENCE South along building line of two-story brick building and West line of Lot 12 a distance of 80.00 ft. to corner;

THENCE East along building line a distance of 23.10 ft. to corner of brick building in the West line of South Main Street;

THENCE North along building line and West line of South Main Street a distance of 74.00 ft. to building corner and continuing North a total distance of 80.00 ft. to Northeast corner of Lot 12, Block D;

THENCE West along the North line of Lot 12, Block D at brick building corner and continuing West along building line a total distance of 23.10 ft. to the PLACE OF BEGINNING;

and containing a total of 1848.00 square feet of land, more or less; being the same tract of land conveyed to Sherman Bailey by Edward Hall on May 28, 1982, recorded in Vol. 1516, Pg. 650, Deed Records of Dallas County, Texas.

TO HAVE AND TO HOLD the above described premises, together with all and singular the rights, hereditaments, and appurtenances thereunto and in any manner belonging, unto to the said GRANTEE, and unto GRANTEE's successors and assigns forever; and GRANTOR does hereby bind GRANTOR, GRANTOR'S heirs, executors and administrators, to Warrant and Defend, all and singular the same unto the said GRANTEE, and unto GRANTEE's successors and assigns, against every person whomsoever lawfully claiming, or to claim the same, or any part thereof.

This conveyance is made and accepted subject to the following matters, to the extent same are in effect at this time: Any and all restrictions, covenants, conditions, and easements, if any, relating to the hereinabove described property, but only to the extent they are still in effect, shown of record in the hereinabove mentioned county and state, and to all zoning laws, regulations and ordinances of municipal and/or other governmental authorities, if any, but only to the extent that they are still in effect, relating to the hereinabove described property.

Executed this ___________ day of ______________________, 19__.

____
SHERMAN BAILEY

STATE OF TEXAS §
§
COUNTY OF DALLAS §

This instrument was acknowledged before me on the ______ day of ___________________________, 19__, by SHERMAN BAILEY.

____
Notary Public for the State of Texas

My Commission Expires: _________________________________
Printed Name of Notary

____

UNIT 11—EXERCISE 2

Warranty Deed with Vendor's Lein

(*Instructions:* The following information is to be used to complete the typical real estate forms, which will be furnished to you. These include a Warranty Deed with Vendor's Lien, Deed of Trust, and Deed of Trust Note. It will be necessary to transcribe the dictated information and then transfer the information to the appropriate blanks on the forms. For all documents, use today's date.)

Grantor: John Q. Moore, joined herein by his wife,
  Sally Sue Moore
3921 Colorado, Dallas County, Dallas, Texas 75233

Grantee: Bonnie H. Marshall, a single woman
306 West 31st Street, Dallas County, Dallas, Texas 75231

Consideration: Thirty Thousand Dollars ($30,000.00) cash in hand paid to the Grantor by the Grantee, the receipt of which is hereby acknowledged and confessed and the further consideration of the execution and delivery by Grantee of that one certain Deed of Trust Note of even date herewith, in the principal sum of Thirty-five Thousand Dollars ($35,000.00), bearing interest thereon as stipulated therein, and payable to the order of The Dallas National Bank, Trustee, which has advanced such sum to Grantee at Grantee's special instance and request as part of the purchase money for the property herein conveyed, and in addition to the Vendor's Lien herein retained, said Note is further described in and secured by a Deed of Trust of even date herewith executed and delivered by Grantee to The Dallas National Bank, Trustee, for the benefit of The Dallas National Bank, Trustee.

Property description: All that certain lot or parcel of

land lying and situated in Dallas County, Texas, more fully described as follows:

Lot numbered one (1) in Block numbered fifty (50) of GLENWOOD TENTH ADDITION to the City of Dallas, Dallas County, Texas, as shown by the Map or Plat of Record in Volume 329, Page 299 of the Plat Records of Dallas County, Texas.

Reservation: This conveyance is made and accepted subject to the following matters, to the extent the same are in effect at this time: Any and all restrictions, covenants, conditions and easements, if any, relating to the hereinabove described property, but only to the extent that they are still in effect, shown of record in the hereinabove mentioned County and State, and to all zoning laws, regulations and ordinances of the Municipal and/or other governmental authorities, if any, but only to the extent they are still in effect, relating to the hereinabove described property.

(*Instruction:* Provide a signature line, as follows, above the Acknowledgment)

Executed this __________ day of ______________________, 19__.

____
John Q. Moore

____
Sally Sue Moore

(*Instructions:* Complete the Acknowledgment for John Q. Moore and Sally Sue Moore on today's date. After recording, return to Grantors at their address. Type in the name and address of your attorney.)

DEED OF TRUST

(Today's Date)

Grantor: Bonnie H. Marshall
(same address)

Trustee:
The Dallas National Bank
P. O. Box 26458
Dallas County
Dallas, TX 75201

Beneficiary:
The Dallas National Bank, Trustee
(same as Trustee address above)

Note:

Date: Today's Date

Amount: $35,000

Maker: Bonnie H. Marshall

Payee: The Dallas National Bank, Trustee

Maturity Date: This will be a date 20 years from 10th day of month following today's date (you will need to calculate this date)

Terms of Payments: As set forth in said Note

Property Description same as in Warranty Deed

Prior Liens: None

Other Exceptions:
Same as Reservations in Deed

Prepare signature line above acknowledgment as follows:

Executed this ________ day of ________ (today's date)

____
Bonnie H. Marshall

(Complete acknowledgment for Bonnie H. Marshall.)

DEED OF TRUST NOTE

(At top of Note on left hand side type amount of note, $35,000.00, in numerals. On right hand side, type city, Dallas, and today's date.)

Payee: The Dallas National Bank

Place of Payment: Dallas, County of Dallas

Principal Amount: $35,000.00

Annual Interest: 8% per annum

Terms of Payment: 240 monthly installments of $292.75 each; first installment due 10th day of month following today's date (date to be calculated by student)

Interest if Entire Note Declared Due: 10%

Payment secured by Deed of Trust to The Dallas National Bank, Trustee.

(Signature line at bottom of page)

Executed this ______ day of ________________________, 19__.

____
Bonnie H. Marshall

UNIT 11—EXERCISE 3

Property Description

DESCRIPTION OF THE JOHN Q. MOORE HOMESTEAD

All that certain lot, tract or parcel of land situated in the JOHN WILLIAMS LEAGUE SURVEY, ABSTRACT NO. 761, in the City of Mesquite, Dallas County, Texas, and being a part of a 39.2 acre tract described in a deed to John Q. Moore recorded in Vol. 525, Page 1655 of the Deed Records of Dallas County, Texas, and being more particularly described as follows:

BEGINNING at an iron rod set for corner in the Northerly Right-of-Way Line of Country Club Road (80′ ROW), said point being South 36 deg. 34 min. East, 212.88 feet from the intersection of the Northwest Right-of-Way Line of Country Club Road and the Southeast Right-of-Way Line of Shiloh Road (100′ ROW), the same being the lower Southwest corner of that certain 3.618 acres, more or less, described in that certain Deed of Trust dated June 10, 1987 from David P. Powders and wife, Janie L. Powders, to Paul L. Pasqual, Trustee, for John Q. Moore, recorded in Vol. 113, Page 4099, Deed of Trust Records, Dallas County, Texas;

THENCE North 47 deg. 17 min. East with Powers′ inner West boundary line, a distance of 398.77 feet to an iron rod set for corner;

THENCE North 42 deg. 43 min. West with Powers′ upper

South boundary line, a distance of 211.66 feet to an iron rod set for corner in the Southeast Right-of-Way Line of Shiloh Road;

THENCE Southwesterly along the Southeast Right-of-Way Line of Shiloh Road, a distance of 377 feet to an iron rod at the intersection of the Northwest Right-of-Way Line of Country Club Road and the Southeast Right-of-Way Line of Shiloh Road (100′ ROW);

THENCE South 36 deg. 34 min. East 212.88 feet to the POINT OF BEGINNING, containing 2.591 acres, more or less.

UNIT 12

Criminal Law

This branch of law sets forth the nature, extent, and degree of every act committed or omitted in violation of penal statutes that command or forbid such act and determines the appropriate penalty. Statutes relative to criminal law may be municipal, state, and/or federal.

VOCABULARY

accessory (ăk-sĕs′-ər-ē)	A person who assists the principal but is not present at the time the crime is committed.
accomplice (ə-kŏm′-plĭs)	A person who knowingly assists the principal in commission of the crime.
admission (ăd-mĭsh′-ən)	A voluntary statement confirming certain facts are true; not a confession of guilt.
alibi (ăl′-ə-bī)	Latin, meaning "elsewhere"; an excuse.
arraignment (ə-rān′-mənt)	The appearance by the accused before a court to hear the charges (indictment or information) against him and to enter a guilty or a not-guilty plea.
assault and battery (ə-sôlt′ ənd băt′-ə-rē)	The threat itself and the use of force on or in harming another; assault is the threat, battery is the action.
breaking and entering (brāk′-ĭng ənd ĕn′-tər-ĭng)	Unlawful, forcible entry with the intention of committing a crime therein; burglary.
burglary (bûr′-glə-rē)	The act of breaking and entering with the intention to commit a felony.
confession (kən-fĕsh′-ən)	A voluntary statement admitting commission of a crime.
constructive breaking (kən-strŭk′-tĭv brāk-ĭng)	Breaking and entering by means of fraud, threats, or trickery.

corpus delicti (kôr′-pəs dĭl-ĭk′-tī)	Latin, meaning "the body of a crime." Does not necessarily mean a human body, but rather that material evidence indicates that a crime has been committed.
criminal intent (krĭm′-ə-nəl ĭn-tĕnt′)	A plan or design to commit a crime. Intent is a necessary element for most criminal charges.
felony (fĕl′-ə-nē)	A serious crime punishable by imprisonment or death.
forgery (fôr′-jə-rē)	Alteration of any written document with the intent to defraud.
fraudulent (frô′-jə-lənt)	Deliberate deception, misrepresentation, or trickery intended to deprive another of his rights or property.
habeas corpus (hā′-bē-əs kôr′-pəs)	Latin; a writ ordering someone holding a person to bring the person into court to determine if he is legally held.
homicide (hŏm′-ə-sīd)	The killing of another person, either intentionally or unintentionally.
incarcerate (ĭn-kär′-sə-rāt)	To imprison as a result of due legal process.
indictment (ĭn-dīt′-mənt)	A grand jury's written accusation that the evidence indicates that a crime has been committed and the person charged should be tried.
information (ĭn-fər-mā′-shən)	A prosecuting attorney's written accusation charging a person with a crime.
larceny (lär′-sə-nē)	The theft of another's property.
malice aforethought (măl′-ĭs ə-fôr′-thôt)	The predetermined intent to commit an unlawful act; one of the elements necessary to prove murder.
manslaughter (măn′-slô-tər)	Unpremeditated killing of another person; may be either voluntary or involuntary.
misdemeanor (mĭs-dĭ-mē′-nər)	Any crime that is not classified as a felony; usually punishable by fine and/or incarceration other than in a penitentiary.
murder (mûr′-dər)	Intentional killing of another person with malice aforethought (premeditation).
nolo contendere (nō′-lō kən-tĕn′-də-rē)	Latin, meaning "I do not wish to contend"; a plea that means the defendant will accept punishment but does not admit guilt.
principal (prĭn′-sə-pəl)	The person who actually commits the crime or aids and abets in its commission.
reasonable doubt (rē′-zən-ə-bəl dout)	Doubt that is reasonable, logical, and/or plausible.
recognizance (rĭ-kŏg′-nə-zəns)	An obligation agreed to in court to do a certain thing.
reprieve (rĭ-prēv′)	A delay or postponement of punishment.

robbery (rŏb′-ər-ē)	The felonious taking of another's property by force or violence.
sentence (sĕn′-təns)	Punishment given by a court to one convicted of a crime.
warrant (wôr′-ənt)	A written authorization (order) to arrest a person or search and/or seize property; issued by a court.

VOCABULARY—DICTATION

A written authorization (or order) to arrest a person or search and/or seize property is referred to as a warrant and is issued by a court. An accomplice is a person who knowingly assists the principal in commission of the crime. A person who assists the principal but is not present at the time the crime is committed is an accessory, either before or after the fact (the crime). In criminal law, the principal is the person who actually commits the crime or aids and abets in its commission.

A voluntary statement confirming that certain facts are true is called an admission; it is not necessarily a confession of guilt. An alibi (Latin, meaning "elsewhere") is an excuse. A voluntary statement admitting commission of a crime is a confession. Recognizance is an obligation agreed to in court to do a certain thing; it is usually used in the expression "released on his own recognizance," which means a person is released without bail with his promise to appear for an additional hearing or trial at a specific time.

In criminal law, the term information refers to the prosecuting attorney's written accusation charging a person with a crime. As opposed to the prosecuting attorney's "information," an indictment is a grand jury's written accusation that the evidence indicates a crime has been committed and the person charged should be tried. The arraignment is the appearance by the accused before a court to hear the charges (either indictment or information) against him. After the charges are read, the accused must enter a guilty or a not-guilty plea.

In criminal law, as in most areas of law, there are many Latin terms. One such term is nolo contendere, which means "I do not wish to contend." This plea signifies that the defendant will accept the punishment but does not admit guilt. A writ of habeas corpus is an order issued to someone holding a person to bring the person into court to determine if he is legally held. Corpus delicti literally means "the body of a crime." It does not necessarily mean a human body, but rather that material evidence indicates that a crime has been committed.

Unlawful, forcible entry with the intention of committing a crime therein is termed breaking and entering. This expression usually goes hand and glove with burglary, which is the act of breaking and entering with the intention to commit a felony, usually theft. Constructive breaking is breaking and entering by means of fraud, threats, or trickery. Larceny is the theft of another's property. The alteration of any written document with the intent to defraud is forgery. A fraudulent transaction is one of deliberate deception, misrepresentation, or trickery and is intended to deprive another of his rights or property. Two crimes usually linked together are assault and battery, which relate to the threat to use force and the use of force on or in harming another; assault is the threat, battery is the action.

The plan or design to commit a crime is referred to as criminal intent. Intent is a necessary element for most criminal charges. A misdemeanor is any crime that is not classified as a felony and is usually punishable by fine and/or incarceration other than in a penitentiary.

A felony is a serious crime punishable by imprisonment or death. Robbery is the felonious taking of another's property by force or violence. The unpremeditated killing of another person, which may be either voluntary or involuntary, is manslaughter. The killing of another person, either intentionally or unintentionally, is homicide. The intentional killing of another person with malice aforethought (premeditation) is murder.

If one is imprisoned as a result of due legal process, he is said to be incarcerated. One of the charges to a jury in a criminal trial is to find if there is reasonable doubt—doubt that is reasonable, logical, and/or plausible. A reprieve is a delay or postponement of punishment. Punishment given by a court to one convicted of a crime is referred to as the sentence.

SELF-TEST—UNIT 12

1. A writ of ________________________ is an order issued to someone holding a person to bring the person into court to determine if he is legally held.
2. A(n) ________________________ is a person who knowingly assists the principal in commission of the crime.
3. Unlawful, forcible entry with the intention of committing a crime therein is ________________________.
4. In criminal law, the ________________________ is the person who actually commits the crime or aids and abets in its commission.
5. A(n) ________________________ is a serious crime punishable by imprisonment or death.
6. A(n) ________________________ is any crime that is not classified as a felony and is usually punishable by fine and/or jail sentence in a county jail.
7. A(n) ________________________ (Latin, meaning "elsewhere") is an excuse.
8. The killing of another person, either intentionally or unintentionally, is ________________________.
9. A voluntary statement admitting commission of a crime is a(n) ________________________.

10. In criminal law, the term ________________________ refers to the prosecuting attorney's written accusation charging a person with a crime.
11. A voluntary statement confirming that certain facts are true is called a(n) ________________________; it is not necessarily a confession of guilt.
12. A(n) ________________________ is a grand jury's written accusation that the evidence indicates that a crime has been committed and the person charged should be tried.
13. Written authorization (or order) to arrest a person or search and/or seize property is referred to as a(n) ________________________ and is issued by a court.
14. Punishment given by the court to one convicted of a crime is referred to as the ________________________.
15. ________________________ literally means "the body of a crime."
16. If one is imprisoned as a result of due legal process, he is said to be ______ ________________.
17. The plan or design to commit a crime is referred to as ___________ ___________.
18. ________________________ is an obligation agreed to in court to do a certain thing.
19. ________________________ is breaking and entering by means of fraud, threats, or trickery.
20. The ________________________ is an appearance by the accused before a court to hear the charges against him (either indictment or information) and to enter a guilty or a not-guilty plea.
21. ________________________ is the theft of another's property.
22. A person who assists the principal but is not present at the time the crime is

committed is a(n) ______________________, either before or after the fact (the crime).

23. Two crimes usually linked together are ______________________, referring to the threat itself and the use of force on or in harming another.
24. ______________________ which means "I do not wish to contend," is a plea that signifies that the defendant will accept the punishment but does not admit guilt.
25. The unpremeditated killing of another person, which may be either voluntary or involuntary, is ______________________.
26. A(n) ______________________ is a delay or postponement of punishment.
27. The intentional killing of another person with malice aforethought (premeditation) is ______________________.
28. ______________________ in a criminal trial is doubt that is reasonable, logical, and/or plausible.
29. A(n) ______________________ transaction is one of deliberate deception, misrepresentation, or trickery and is intended to deprive another of his rights or property.
30. ______________________ is the felonious taking of another's property by force or violence.
31. The alteration of any written document with the intent to defraud is ______________________.
32. The act of breaking and entering with the intention to commit a felony, usually theft, is ______________________.
33. One of the elements required to prove murder is the predetermined intent to commit an unlawful act, which is referred to as ______________________.

UNIT 12—EXERCISE 1

Motion to Suppress (Search)

(*Instructions:* The caption or style for all exercises in Unit 12 will be the same.)

No. 28567

THE STATE OF TEXAS	§	IN THE DISTRICT COURT
	§	
v.	§	147TH JUDICIAL DISTRICT
	§	
JOHN Q. MOORE, JR.	§	DALLAS COUNTY, TEXAS

MOTION TO SUPPRESS

TO THE HONORABLE JUDGE OF SAID COURT:

The Defendant, John Q. Moore, Jr., by and through his counsel respectfully moves this Honorable Court to suppress all evidence seized as the result of a search of the following premises: 1989 Pontiac Bonneville, Texas License No. 583-BDX, on the __________ day of ___________________________, A.D. 19__, and the search of the person of the Defendant, and all statements either written or oral made after the arrest of the Defendant.

The Defendant relies upon the following reasons to support aforesaid motion.

I.

That the Defendant was arrested without warrant and without probable cause in violation of the IV, V, and XIV Amendments to the Constitution of the United States.

II.

That the search of his person and the premises in question incident to such arrest was therefore illegal and all the fruits of the search must be suppressed.

III.

That if such arrest or search were upon an arrest warrant or a search warrant, the affidavit therefor did not allege sufficient facts to establish probable cause.

IV.

All statements either written or oral made after his, the said Defendant's, arrest are fruits of the illegal arrest and search and are therefore inadmissible as fruits of the poisonous tree.

Respectfully submitted,

Signature block for Attorney
for Defendant

UNIT 12—EXERCISE 2

Motion to Suppress (Polygraph)

No. 28567

THE STATE OF TEXAS	§	IN THE DISTRICT COURT
	§	
v.	§	147TH JUDICIAL DISTRICT
	§	
JOHN Q. MOORE, JR.	§	DALLAS COUNTY, TEXAS

MOTION TO SUPPRESS

TO THE HONORABLE JUDGE OF SAID COURT:

NOW COMES the Defendant herein, John Q. Moore, Jr., joined by his attorney of record, and files this motion with the court and in support of said motion would show unto the Court as follows:

I.

Movants would show unto the Court that the results of a polygraph or lie detector test are inadmissible in the courts of Texas, and that the refusal of an accused to take a polygraph or lie detector test is inadmissible and prejudicial to the rights of this Defendant in obtaining a fair and impartial trial before the jury.

II.

Movants would further show, should it have occurred that the police officers offered the Defendant herein a polygraph or lie detector test and that he refused such test, which is not admitted, that testimony regarding offering any test while the Defendant was under arrest and in police custody and the refusal of the taking of any such test, if such was refused, would be prejudicial and damaging to this Defendant.

WHEREFORE, PREMISES CONSIDERED, movants pray that the state not be allowed to elicit before the jury that the Defendant was offered a polygraph or lie detector test by the police officers, if he was, and that the Defendant refused such test, if he did, for the reason that same would be prejudicial and damaging to the rights of the Defendant before the jury and prejudicial to his obtaining a fair trial.

Respectfully submitted,

____
John Q. Moore, Jr., Defendant

Signature Block for Attorney for Defendant

Granted.

Refused, to which the Defendant excepts.

____
Judge Presiding

UNIT 12—EXERCISE 3

Waiver of Speedy Trial

No. 28567

THE STATE OF TEXAS	§	IN THE DISTRICT COURT
	§	
v.	§	147TH JUDICIAL DISTRICT
	§	
JOHN Q. MOORE, JR.	§	DALLAS COUNTY, TEXAS

WAIVER OF SPEEDY TRIAL

TO THE HONORABLE JUDGE OF SAID COURT:

NOW COMES the Defendant in the above-entitled and numbered cause, represented by his attorney of record, and states that his attorney has advised him of his rights under the Speedy Trial Act, but that he voluntarily and knowingly waives such rights and agrees that this case be called for trial without regard to the requirements of the Speedy Trial Act.

Respectfully submitted,

____

Defendant

Signature Block for Attorney for Defendant

UNIT 12—EXERCISE 4

Motion to Try Issue of Mental Competency

No. 28567

THE STATE OF TEXAS	§	IN THE DISTRICT COURT
	§	
v.	§	147TH JUDICIAL DISTRICT
	§	
JOHN Q. MOORE, JR.	§	DALLAS COUNTY, TEXAS

MOTION TO TRY ISSUE OF MENTAL COMPETENCY

TO THE HONORABLE JUDGE OF SAID COURT:

NOW COMES the attorney for the Defendant, John Q. Moore, Jr., and, prior to the date set for trial on the merits, files this written application on behalf of the Defendant and would respectfully show the following:

That the Defendant is mentally incompetent at this time to stand trial in that the Defendant does not have sufficient present ability to consult with his attorney with a reasonable degree of rational understanding and does not have a rational, as well as a factual, understanding of the proceedings against him.

WHEREFORE, it is prayed on behalf of Defendant that, in advance of the trial on the merits, a trial be had on the issue of Defendant's competency to stand trial at the present time.

Respectfully submitted,

____

Signature block for Attorney for Defendant

UNIT 12—EXERCISE 5

Order Granting Motion to Try Issue of Mental Competency

No. 28567

THE STATE OF TEXAS	§	IN THE DISTRICT COURT
	§	
v.	§	147TH JUDICIAL DISTRICT
	§	
JOHN Q. MOORE, JR.	§	DALLAS COUNTY, TEXAS

ORDER

On this ________ day of ____________________, 19__, A.D. came on to be heard Motion of the Attorney for the Defendant to try the issue of mental competency before a trial on the merits of the case; and it appearing that the Defendant is entitled to the relief sought.

IT IS THEREFORE, ORDERED that this case be set for a trial before a jury on the ________ day of ________________, 19__, A.D., on the issue of the Defendant's mental competency to stand trial on the merits of the case.

____
Judge Presiding

UNIT 12—EXERCISE 6

Petition for Writ of Habeas Corpus

No. 28567

THE STATE OF TEXAS	§	IN THE DISTRICT COURT
	§	
v.	§	147TH JUDICIAL DISTRICT
	§	
JOHN Q. MOORE, JR.	§	DALLAS COUNTY, TEXAS

PETITION FOR WRIT OF HABEAS CORPUS

TO THE HONORABLE JUDGE OF SAID COURT:

NOW COMES John Q. Moore, Jr., hereinafter called Applicant, by and through Michelle Underwood, his Attorney and Petitioner herein, and files this her petition and application for writ of habeas corpus and would show the Court the following:

I.

That Applicant is illegally confined and restrained of his liberty by the Sheriff of Dallas County, in the County Jail, located in the City of Dallas, Dallas County, Texas.

II.

Said confinement and restraint is not by virtue of any writ, order or process, and no probable cause exists for the detention of said Applicant but is wholly illegal and unlawful.

WHEREFORE, PREMISES CONSIDERED, Petitioner prays that this Court grant and issue a Writ of Habeas Corpus to the said Sheriff of Dallas County directing and commanding him to produce and have Applicant before this Court instanter, or at such time and place to be by this Court designated, then and there to show cause, if any he may have, why Applicant should not be discharged from such illegal confinement and restraint.

Respectfully submitted,

____

Signature Block for Attorney for Applicant

UNIT 12—EXERCISE 7

Order Granting Writ and Setting Hearing

No. 28567

THE STATE OF TEXAS	§	IN THE DISTRICT COURT
	§	
v.	§	147TH JUDICIAL DISTRICT
	§	
JOHN Q. MOORE, JR.	§	DALLAS COUNTY, TEXAS

ORDER GRANTING WRIT AND SETTING HEARING

On this ________ day of ____________________, 19__, came on to be heard the petition for Writ of Habeas Corpus by Applicant, John Q. Moore, Jr., and the Court having considered the same finds that the writ should be issued and Applicant granted an evidentiary hearing.

IT IS THEREFORE ORDERED, ADJUDGED and DECREED that a writ be issued directing the Respondent to produce Applicant before the 147th Judicial District Court of Dallas County, Texas, on the ________ day of ____________________, 19__ at ________ o'clock ____. M. for a hearing to determine whether Applicant is entitled to the relief sought.

____
Judge Presiding

APPENDIX A

Answers to Self-Tests

UNIT 1

1. whereas
2. albeit
3. bankruptcy
4. adjudicated
5. Law
6. tortfeasor
7. legal
8. therefore
9. precedent
10. citation; cite
11. allegation
12. common law
13. jurisprudence; jurist
14. case law
15. hereunto
16. constitutional law
17. statutory law
18. Court; the Bar
19. forthwith
20. counsel
21. therefor
22. plaintiff; defendant
23. in propria persona; in pro per
24. execute
25. per se
26. feasance
27. heretofore
28. malfeasance
29. mandatory
30. misfeasance & nonfeasance
31. tort
32. thereby

UNIT 2

1. Justice of the Peace Court
2. Probate Court
3. Municipal Court
4. County Court
5. County Court at Law
6. District Court
7. Criminal District Court
8. Court of Appeals
9. Court of Criminal Appeals
10. Texas Supreme Court
11. U.S. District Court
12. U.S. Court of Appeals
13. U.S. Supreme Court
14. dictum

UNIT 3

1. venue
2. affidavit
3. above-entitled
4. affiant
5. jurisdiction
6. et alius
7. acknowledgment
8. endorsement
9. prayer
10. jurat
11. in re
12. certificate of service
13. verification
14. above-named
15. caption or style

UNIT 4A

1. counterclaim
2. petition
3. Tangible damages
4. citation
5. answer
6. grounds for
7. pleadings
8. default
9. at issue
10. contributory negligence
11. conformed
12. court docket
13. Personal service
14. proximate cause
15. docket number
16. cross-claim
17. statute of limitations
18. litigant

UNIT 4B

1. disclosure
2. subpoena duces tecum
3. deposition
4. enjoin
5. motion
6. res ipsa loquitur
7. subpoena
8. interrogatories

UNIT 5

1. peremptory challenges
2. perjury
3. mistrial
4. rebuttal
5. evidence
6. voir dire
7. plenary trial
8. testimony
9. immaterial
10. quash
11. hearsay
12. exhibit
13. admissible
14. irrelevent
15. impeach
16. corroborative
17. challenge for cause

UNIT 6

1. with prejudice
2. stare decisis
3. pendente lite
4. order
5. nonsuit
6. without prejudice

7. interlocutory
8. writ
9. opinion
10. summary judgment
11. charge to the jury
12. verdict
13. restraining order
14. acquittal
15. Prima facie
16. exonerated
17. Res judicata
18. irreparable
19. deliberations
20. contempt of court
21. jointly and severally
22. judgment
23. decree
24. Per curiam
25. sequestered

UNIT 7

1. Mandamus
2. transcript
3. Compensatory damages
4. appellant
5. injunction
6. appeal
7. writ of certiorari
8. stay
9. brief
10. damages
11. trial de novo
12. redress
13. Amicus curiae
14. supersedeas
15. appellee
16. reversed
17. abrogate
18. remanded

UNIT 8

1. desertion
2. privileged communications
3. common-law marriage
4. annulment
5. void marriage
6. custody
7. voidable marriage
8. irreconcilable
9. Separate maintenance
10. community property
11. Divorce
12. valid marriage
13. Alimony pendente lite
14. separate property
15. petitioner
16. antenuptial agreement
17. corespondent
18. separation
19. respondent
20. cohabitation
21. adoption

UNIT 9A

1. testimonium clause
2. intestate
3. holographic will
4. testamentary capacity
5. estate
6. testator; testatrix
7. codicil
8. Per stirpes
9. nuncupative will
10. will
11. attestation clause
12. residue

UNIT 9B

1. Chattels
2. executor; executrix
3. administrator cum testamento annexo
4. residuary estate
5. Precatory words
6. muniment of title
7. conservator
8. bequeath
9. Probate
10. bequest
11. hereditaments
12. administrator; administratrix
13. Escheat
14. guardian
15. beneficiary
16. devise
17. trust
18. Guardian ad litem
19. heir
20. ward

UNIT 10A

1. general partner
2. partnership
3. proprietor
4. power of attorney
5. limited partner

UNIT 10B

1. Dividends
2. subsidiary
3. Retained earnings
4. charter
5. liability
6. domestic corporation
7. corporation
8. franchise
9. alien corporation
10. legal entity
11. Liquidation
12. merger
13. eleemosynary corporation
14. foreign corporation
15. proxy
16. asset
17. bylaws
18. articles of incorporation
19. net worth
20. Dissolution
21. quorum

UNIT 10C

1. performance
2. contract
3. surety
4. option
5. caveat emptor
6. competent parties
7. vitiate
8. Consideration
9. rescind
10. Collateral
11. Quid pro quo
12. breach of contract
13. executed
14. offer
15. Subrogation
16. Acceptance
17. escalator clause
18. covenant
19. indemnify

UNIT 11

1. warranty deed
2. abstract
3. plat
4. encumbrance
5. mortgagee
6. Title
7. deed
8. grantee
9. fixture
10. homestead
11. Domain
12. mortgage note
13. grantor
14. possession
15. real property
16. mortgagor
17. quitclaim deed
18. appurtenance
19. Eminent domain
20. Conveyance
21. joint tenancy
22. escrow
23. hypothecates
24. condemnation
25. fee simple
26. lien
27. Recording
28. lessor
29. assessment
30. easement
31. conveyed
32. Public domain
33. foreclosure
34. adverse possession
35. lessee
36. notice to quit
37. ad valorem
38. eviction
39. amortized

UNIT 12

1. habeas corpus
2. accomplice
3. breaking and entering
4. principal
5. felony
6. misdemeanor
7. alibi
8. homicide
9. confession
10. information
11. admission
12. indictment
13. warrant
14. sentence
15. Corpus delicti
16. incarcerated
17. criminal intent
18. Recognizance
19. Constructive breaking
20. arraignment
21. Larceny
22. accessory
23. assault and battery
24. Nolo contendere
25. manslaughter
26. reprieve
27. murder
28. Reasonable doubt
29. fraudulent
30. Robbery
31. forgery
32. burglary
33. malice aforethought

APPENDIX B

Style and Format Samples

LETTER—STANDARD

SUTTON, UNDERWOOD & EDWARDS
10375 Merriman Parkway
Dallas, Texas 75231

Bruce R. Sutton **(214) 349-8783**
Michelle L. Underwood **Fax (214) 346-6639**
Robert B. Edwards

Date

Robert P. Brown, Esq.
Brown, Rogers, & Smith
Attorneys at Law
P.O. Box 6294
Dallas, TX 75253

Re: No. 89-22543
El Dorado Partners vs.
Dallas Central Appraisal
District et al.

Dear Mr. Brown:

At the conclusion of the meeting with the Appraisal District officials on August 30, 1995, Mr. Roy Lawson advised the group that he would recompute values in the form of an appraisal and submit the same within three weeks. I would appreciate your furnishing us with a copy of this calculation or appraisal report as soon as you receive the same.

Your attention and consideration in this matter will be appreciated.

Very truly yours,

Bruce R. Sutton

BS:mw

LETTER—MODIFIED BLOCK

SUTTON, UNDERWOOD & EDWARDS
10375 Merriman Parkway
Dallas, Texas 75231

Bruce R. Sutton **(214) 349-8783**
Michelle L. Underwood **Fax (214) 346-6639**
Robert B. Edwards

Date

Mr. Robert P. Brown
Brown, Rogers, & Smith
Attorneys at Law
P.O. Box 6294
Dallas, TX 75253

Re: No. 89-22543
El Dorado Partners vs.
Dallas Central Appraisal
District et al.

Dear Mr. Brown:

At the conclusion of the meeting with the Appraisal District officials on August 30, 1995, Mr. Roy Lawson advised the group that he would recompute values in the form of an appraisal and submit the same within three weeks. I would appreciate your furnishing us with a copy of this calculation or appraisal report as soon as you receive the same.

Your attention and consideration in this matter will be appreciated.

Very truly yours,

Bruce R. Sutton

BS:mw

LETTER—BLOCK

SUTTON, UNDERWOOD & EDWARDS
10375 Merriman Parkway
Dallas, Texas 75231

Bruce R. Sutton **(214) 349-8783**
Michelle L. Underwood **Fax (214) 346-6639**
Robert B. Edwards

Date

Robert P. Brown, Esq.
Brown, Rogers, & Smith
Attorneys at Law
P.O. Box 6294
Dallas, TX 75253

Re: No. 89-22543
El Dorado Partners vs.
Dallas Central Appraisal
District et al.

Dear Mr. Brown:

At the conclusion of the meeting with the Appraisal District officials on August 30, 1995, Mr. Roy Lawson advised the group that he would recompute values in the form of an appraisal and submit the same within three weeks. I would appreciate your furnishing us with a copy of this calculation or appraisal report as soon as you receive the same.

Your attention and consideration in this matter will be appreciated.

Very truly yours,

Bruce R. Sutton

BS:mw

DISTRICT COURT CAPTION

No. ________________

FLOWER COUNTRY CLUB, INC.,	§	IN THE DISTRICT COURT
	§	
Plaintiff,	§	
	§	
vs.	§	
	§	109TH JUDICIAL DISTRICT
DALLAS COUNTY APPRAISAL DISTRICT	§	
and APPRAISAL REVIEW BOARD	§	
OF DALLAS COUNTY APPRAISAL	§	
DISTRICT,	§	
	§	
Defendants.	§	DALLAS COUNTY, TEXAS

PLAINTIFF'S ORIGINAL PETITION

TO THE HONORABLE JUDGE OF THE SAID COURT:

NOW COMES, Flower Country Club, Plaintiff herein, and brings this suit against Dallas County Appraisal District and Appraisal Review Board of Dallas County Appraisal District, Defendants herein, and for cause of action would respectfully show the Court as follows.

I.

WHEREFORE, PREMISES CONSIDERED, Plaintiff prays that

Respectfully submitted,

____

MICHELLE L. UNDERWOOD
State Bar ID No. 10933090

10375 Merriman Parkway
Dallas, Texas 75231
(214) 349-8783
(214) 340-7643 (Fax)

ATTORNEY FOR PLAINTIFF

ORIGINAL PETITION—Page 1

SIGNATURE BLOCK

Documents filed with the court usually close with "Respectfully submitted," a line for signature, attorney name and State Bar number, address, telephone number, fax number and designation as to the party (plaintiff or defendant) represented by the attorney (or firm).

Respectfully submitted,

____

MICHELLE L. UNDERWOOD
State Bar ID No. 10933090

10375 Merriman Parkway
Dallas, Texas 75231
(214) 349-8783
(214) 340-7643 (Fax)

ATTORNEY FOR PLAINTIFF

(*Note:* Whether the name of the attorney and the designation Attorney for Plantiff are all caps or upper- and lowercase is totally a matter of preference of the attorney—there is no set rule.)

CERTIFICATE OF SERVICE

After the Original Petition has been filed and served on the defendant(s), all legal documents (starting with Defendant's Original Answer) relative to the lawsuit that are filed with the court must include (at the end of the document) a Certificate of Service, which certifies that all parties to the suit have been furnished a copy of the document. The form of the certificate may vary but must include either the title of the document or reference to it (e.g., "the foregoing document"), the name of the party or parties being furnished a copy, and the date mailed or delivered.

CERTIFICATE OF SERVICE

This is to certify that a true and correct copy of Defendant's Original Answer has been served by Certified Mail No. ____________________, Return Receipt Requested, upon Plaintiff's Attorney of Record addressed as follows:

Mr. Richard F. Smith
Abrams, Forest, Preston & Spring
2800 Lincoln Plaza
500 N. Akard
Dallas, Texas 75201

on this ____________ day of ______________________, 19__.

____
Michelle L. Underwood

SIMPLE NOTARY

STATE OF TEXAS §
§
COUNTY OF DALLAS §

Subscribed and sworn to before me, the undersigned authority, this ______ day of ________________________, 19__.

____
Notary Public, State of Texas

My commission expires:

____
Printed Name of Notary

____

JURAT

Quite often attorneys will dictate: "Add a subscribed and sworn to." This is an addition to the end of the instrument whereby the Notary Public takes the subscriber's oath that the foregoing document is true. It is signed by the subscriber and attested to by the Notary.

STATE OF TEXAS §
§
COUNTY OF DALLAS §

BEFORE ME, the undersigned authority, on this day personally appeared John Roe, who being by me duly sworn, deposed and said that he is the Attorney of Record for Valium, Inc.; that he has read the above and foregoing Defendant's Original Answer, and that the statements contained therein are within his personal knowledge true and correct.

____
John Roe

SUBSCRIBED AND SWORN TO BEFORE ME, the undersigned authority, on this _______ day of ____________________, 19__.

____
Notary Public, State of Texas

My commission expires:

____
Printed Name of Notary

____

ACKNOWLEDGMENT

An *acknowledgment* is a statement made under oath by the person(s) whose signature(s) appears on the document that he/she/they executed the document. The most common use of the acknowledgment is on real estate documents.

STATE OF TEXAS §
§
COUNTY OF DALLAS §

This instrument was acknowledged before me on the ______

day of __________________, 19__ by _________________________

and ____.

____
Notary Public, State of Texas

My commission expires:

____
Notary's Printed Name

____

CAPTION FOR STATE COURT OF APPEALS

No. 08-90-00432-CV

IN THE COURT OF APPEALS
8TH DISTRICT OF TEXAS
EL PASO, TEXAS

GENERAL EQUITY LEASING CORPORATION,

Appellant,

V.

LUBBOCK CENTRAL APPRAISAL DISTRICT and
APPRAISAL REVIEW BOARD OF LUBBOCK CENTRAL APPRAISAL DISTRICT,

Appellees.

ON APPEAL FROM THE 153RD JUDICIAL DISTRICT

COURT OF LUBBOCK COUNTY, TEXAS

BRIEF OF APPELLANT, GENERAL EQUITY LEASING CORPORATION

BRUCE R. SUTTON
State Bar ID No. 10652000

10375 Merriman Parkway
Dallas, Texas 75231
(214) 349-8783

ATTORNEY FOR APPELLANT

CITATIONS

INDEX OF AUTHORITIES

Cases	Page
Adams v. Kendall County Appraisal District, 724 S.W.2d 781 (Tex.App.—San Antonio 1986, no writ)	14
Armstrong v. Manzo, 380 U.S. 545, 85 S.Ct. 1187, 14 L.Ed.2d 62 (1965)	9
Austin National Bank v. Sheppard, 71 S.W.2d 242 (Com.App. 1934, opinion adopted)	28
Constitutions	
United States Constitution, 14th Amendment, Section 1	10
Texas Constitution, Art. I, Section 13	13, 15
Statutes	
Texas Property Tax Code, Chapters 41 and 42	30
Texas Property Tax Code, Section 21.02	20, 21, 22, 23

FEDERAL COURT CAPTION

IN THE UNITED STATES DISTRICT COURT
FOR THE NORTHERN DISTRICT OF TEXAS
DALLAS DIVISION

```
ABC Company,*                    §
                                 §
    Plaintiff,                   §
                                 §
vs.                              § CIVIL ACTION NO. ________
                                 §
XYZ Corporation, John Doe,       §
individually, and Doe Brothers,  §
a Partnership,                   §
                                 §
    Defendants.                  §
```

<u>COMPLAINT</u>

(Body of Complaint)

Respectfully submitted,

____
Robert Roe

Address
Telephone Number
Fax Number

ATTORNEY FOR PLAINTIFF*

(*Note:* * Whether all caps or upper- and lowercase for caption is attorney preference and firm policy.)

LAST WILL AND TESTAMENT

LAST WILL AND TESTAMENT
OF
ROBERT ROE

STATE OF TEXAS §
§ KNOW ALL MEN BY THESE PRESENTS:
COUNTY OF DALLAS §

That I, ROBERT ROE, a resident of Dallas County, State of Texas, being in good health, of sound and disposing mind and memory and above the age of eighteen (18) years, do hereby make and publish this my Last Will and Testament, hereby revoking all wills made by me heretofore at any time.

ARTICLE ONE

ATTESTATION CLAUSE

STATE OF TEXAS §
§
COUNTY OF DALLAS §

BEFORE ME, the undersigned authority, on this day personally appeared Robert Roe, ____________________ and ____________________, known to me to be the Testator and the Witnesses, respectively, whose names are subscribed to the annexed or foregoing instrument in their respective capacities. All of these persons being duly sworn by me, Robert Roe, the Testator, declared to me and to the Witnesses in my presence that this instrument is his Will and he had willing made and executed it as his free act and deed for the purposes expressed in it. The Witnesses, each under oath, stated to me in the presence and hearing of the Testator that the Testator declared to them that this instrument is his Will and that he executed it as such and wanted each of them to sign it as a witness. The Witnesses also stated under oath that they signed the instrument as witnesses in the presence of the Testator at his request, that the Testator was at that time at least eighteen (18) years of age and was of sound mind and that each of the witnesses was at that time at least fourteen (14) years of age.

____
ROBERT ROE, Testator

____
Witness

____
Witness

SUBSCRIBED AND ACKNOWLEDGED BEFORE ME by the said Robert Roe, Testator, and SUBSCRIBED AND SWORN TO BEFORE ME by the said ____________________ and ____________________, witnesses, this ______ day of ____________________, 19__.

____
Notary Public, State of Texas

My Commission Expires:

____
Printed Name of Notary

____

APPENDIX C

Index to Vocabulary

W